APPALACHIAN HERITAGE

VOL. 43, NO. 2
SPRING 2015

ESTABLISHED IN 1973

PUBLISHED QUARTERLY
by Berea College
CPO 2166
205 N. Main Street
Berea, KY, 40404

www.appalachianheritage.net

 Periodicals postage paid at Berea, Kentucky, and at additional mailing offices. ISSN# 03632318.

Electronic submissions only at www.appalachianheritage.net

Distributed by the University of North Carolina Press. Basic subscription price: $30/year for individuals, $40/year for institutions. For subscription requests and inquiries, visit the magazine's website, email uncpress_journals@unc.edu, or call 919.962.4201.

CONTENTS

INTERVIEW

CRAFT ESSAY

BOOK REVIEWS

COVER PHOTOGRAPH

EDITOR'S NOTE

JASON HOWARD

Since February, three friends of mine have been diagnosed with cancer. Their stories are all too familiar. A few odd pains—nothing too severe—an eventual doctor's visit, followed by a couple more, and finally, a diagnosis that seemingly came from out of the blue. They are all in their sixties. Far too young.

One occupied a large space in the landscape of my childhood. He bought me my first guitar, gave me my first beer, taught me about country music—about Hank Williams, Patsy Cline, George Jones, and Tammy Wynette. One time he was listening to Patsy sing "Faded Love," and he pulled me over to the stereo. "Listen to this, Jason," he said. "Listen to the breath she takes before she goes for that last note." He pointed at the speakers, and indeed there it was, Patsy's vulnerability on full display for the close listener, a moment of beauty that he had not missed.

In thinking of him over the past couple of months, I keep remembering a song he used to sing about someone being kept up at night by a memory that refuses to be silenced. It's a sentiment that I believe many of the contributors to this issue would recognize, as so many of these stories, essays, and poems are rooted in memory—in having, as Michael Ondaatje writes in *The Cat's Table*, "an old knot in the heart we wish to untie."

Such heartstrings are on full display in "When You Say 'Home,'" a new short story by bestselling novelist Wiley Cash, who is also interviewed in these pages by Amy D. Clark. The knots are present in stories by emerging writers Natalie Sypolt and Devin Kelly, each of whom ground their work in stark beauty and lyricism; in aching pieces of flash nonfiction by acclaimed fiction writer Holly Goddard Jones and essayist Laura Michele Diener; in poems whose subjects range from hawks in flight, bus stop encounters, immigration, and family politics. They can even be found in Genevieve Thurtle's engaging craft essay "Tragedy on a Large Stage," which explores the setting of Vietnam in Tim O'Brien's classic short story "How to Tell a True War Story" and how "the slippery nature of narrative truth becomes even more so when memory comes into play."

Bear witness as these wonderful writers begin to untie the old knots in their hearts. Keep your eyes and ears peeled for moments of beauty, for wistful breaths like the one Patsy took. And like my old friend, pause to savor them. ■

WHEN YOU SAY "HOME"

WILEY CASH

I've got a whole mess of stuff to do today," Michael's mother said. He watched her reach up into the hallway closet and pull their big, red suitcase from the top shelf. Michael's grandmother was being turned out of another nursing home, this one just down Highway 74 towards King's Mountain.

Michael had overheard his mother on the kitchen phone the day before.

"She said that?" she'd asked. "To Renee?" Michael had walked into the kitchen just as his mother was hanging up the phone. She crossed her arms and leaned up against the counter.

"Your grandmama's calling people the inward again," she'd said. She rubbed her eyes with both hands. "I thought we'd gotten past that one."

Now Michael watched his mother carry the empty red suitcase into the living room and set it down beside the front door as if it had been packed for him and was waiting there to be picked up and carried outside once Laura showed up.

"It'll be good for you and Laura to spend some time together," his mother said. "I think it'll be nice." She moved the blinds apart and looked out the window as if already expecting Laura's truck to be in the driveway. "Besides," she said, "it's important for everybody to be friends." She looked at Michael and smiled.

But Michael didn't really want to be friends with Laura. He was only eight years old, but he figured eight was plenty old enough to understand the world, at least the world as it made itself understood in Shelby, North Carolina. He understood that his mom wanted him to be friends with Laura only because she'd been coming around a lot lately, but Michael had a long memory—even at eight years old—of all kinds of people coming around since the two of them had moved to town that fall. The one Michael had liked best was a guy named Travis who seemed a good bit younger than Michael's mother and who traveled around painting water towers. He'd told Michael that he'd even painted a water tower that was made to look like a giant peach down in Gaffney, South Carolina. Michael didn't believe such a thing could exist until Travis pulled out his cell phone and flipped it open and showed Michael a picture of that water tower that had been taken from the side of the interstate, the bright orange skin of the peach peeking out above the trees. He figured anybody could've pulled over and taken that picture, but he'd never seen anything like it before, and it gave him something to think about: Travis scaling the face of that peach, holding onto a rope or a rope holding onto him—however such a thing could be done—an orange-tipped paintbrush in his hand.

It had only been nine months since they'd moved west from Fayetteville where Michael's dad was still living on the base at Camp LeJeune, but only if he wasn't back in Iraq or Afghanistan or one of the other places he'd spent so much time while Michael was growing up. They'd come to Shelby because it was where his mother had been raised and where his grandmother still lived. Michael's mother had told him that when she was a kid everybody had called her Jolene, even though her name was Jodi. She went by Jodi now, and she made clear that anybody who was somebody in Shelby would remember her by that name only. "But why'd they call you Jolene if it isn't your name?" he'd asked. His mother had sighed and looked out the car window toward the blue ridges farther west. "Because," she'd said. "That's what boys do. At least the boys in Shelby."

Now Michael stood outside his mother's bathroom, leaning up against the doorframe and watching her curl her hair with one hand and mist hairspray on it with the other. When she released a strand from the curler her hair hardly moved.

"Why can't I just go with you to the nursing home?" he asked.

"Because I can't keep an eye on you and your grandmother at the same time. Y'all will just wander off in different directions, and I won't know who to chase after first."

"I won't wander off," he said. "I promise." The worst he'd ever done was leave the room and wander down the hall one afternoon while his mother met with the staff and his grandmother argued with her roommate, a leathery, angry old woman who everybody called Little Mama.

"She's a day older than the devil," Michael's grandmother had whispered loud enough for her voice to be heard across the room. "And that extra day didn't do nothing but make her meaner. And she keeps stealing my magazines."

Little Mama had been sitting in her recliner, watching soap operas with the volume turned all the way down.

"She's only got it turned down because she wants to hear our business," Michael's grandmother had said.

Little Mama's silence had seemed to suggest she'd absorbed the comments or just hadn't heard it, but a moment later she turned her head and stared at Michael's grandmother.

"I don't give a damn shit what you're saying," she'd said. "I got the volume turned off because I like to make up my own words."

Michael stood outside his mother's bathroom, leaning up against the doorframe and watching her curl her hair with one hand and mist hairspray on it with the other.

Michael knew his mother didn't want him standing around watching her while she packed up Grandma's things and convinced her it was a good idea to split before things got even rougher with Little Mama. He put his hands in the pockets of his jeans and looked out into the living room, toward the front door.

"But what am I supposed to do with Laura while you're gone?" he asked.

"She's got a surprise for you," his mother said, releasing a final curl and fluffing her hair with her fingers. "And I don't want to ruin it—well, not all of it anyway—but I reckon I'll go ahead and tell you one part: She's taking you over to the fair." She looked at Michael and raised her eyebrows like he should already be able to feel the excitement, and that was okay, because he was excited. His mother had taken him out to the dusty fairgrounds not too long after they'd moved to Shelby at the end of the summer. That night she'd bought him all kinds of food and let him ride whichever rickety ride he'd wanted to, and she'd even ridden some of them with him. The only thing she wouldn't let him do was go inside the freak show tent.

"You're not quite old enough for that," she'd said, which had disappointed him then, but it disappointed him even more when he heard a kid in his class named Billy McPherson talk about the pictures of naked ladies that were hanging up inside the tent. He said all the ladies were covered in tattoos—and some of them had scales like fish—but they'd been naked just the same.

But Michael's favorite thing about the fair had been the agricultural shows where hundreds of cows, pigs, sheep, and other kinds of animals he'd only seen through the car's windows were pinned up inside long metal buildings. The night had been hot, and the high-ceilinged halls had carried the soft scents of hay and manure from the showroom and up toward the fans that pulled the heat out of the building. It was April now, just a few weeks past Easter, and Michael figured it wouldn't be hot enough for the fans to be running, but he hoped those buildings would smell the same while he and Laura took their time going from pen to pen, Michael reaching out his hand and touching the pigs' soft, bristly ears and the goats' hard, knobby horns.

"What's the surprise?" Michael asked.

"You'll have to wait and find out," his mother said. "That's why they call it a surprise."

■ ■ ■

While his mother finished getting ready, Michael walked into the living room and looked out the window. The two of them lived in a cul-de-sac that had been nothing but what folks in town called "country" just a decade before. Now the paved road was lined with single-story, three bedroom homes whose vinyl sidings were different shades of tan. The only remnant of "country" was an old, collapsing barn about three hundred yards past the trees in Michael's backyard. The barn's wood had turned dark brown, almost black, and a rusted red corn harvester with broken windows sat beside it. Before they even moved into the house, Michael's mother had taken his hand and led him to the edge of the backyard and pointed through the trees toward the barn.

"I will wear you out if I ever catch you near that place," she promised. "It's dangerous, and you might be killed." She gave him a look that let him know she meant it, even though she'd never spanked him in his entire life. But he listened to her and never went near the barn or the harvester, but that didn't keep him from staring at it when he played in the backyard.

One day at school, during art class, he'd painted a picture of the barn, leaving the harvester out because the paintbrush was too thick to get all of its details right. The art teacher came around and praised each kid's painting, and when she got to Michael's she stared over his shoulder.

"What a pretty barn," she said. "Did you make it up or have you seen it before?"

"It's in my backyard," he said.

"Oh," she said. "You must live out in the country. Not a lot folks in this town know what it's like to have a barn in their yards, not like they used to anyway."

Michael just nodded his head by way of agreement, but inside he felt something blooming: a sense of pride in the place he'd come from—at the least place where he lived now—and for the first time in a long time—maybe for the first time in his life—he could point to a place and say, "This place right here is where I'm from."

■ ■ ■

Michael heard Laura's truck pull into the driveway, and he peered out the blinds again and saw her sitting inside the cab of her truck, finishing a phone call, the huge engine already cooling with loud pops and hisses. Although Michael couldn't see the sign on the truck's door panel because of the way it was parked, he knew what it said: Moss Lake Custom Homes: Pre-Fab Meets Fabulous. A website and a phone number were lettered beneath.

Michael had overheard his mother tell people that her friend Laura was a builder, and although Michael had never seen Laura build anything he had a vague image of her standing in a field where the grass had been tramped down by the wheels of huge trucks, a pile of lumber in front of her: Laura is wearing a tool belt with a hammer hanging at her side and holding a tape measure in her hand. She looks at her watch and stares up toward the sun, and then she gets to work.

Michael watched Laura climb down from her truck and start up the short sidewalk to the house. Laura spoke loudly into her cell phone, so loud that Michael could hear every word.

"I don't give a shit, Charlie," Laura said. "He needs to stick to the script I wrote out." She stopped walking like she was listening intently to someone on the other end. "Well that's why I wrote it out." Laura had on tan lace-up boots and blue jeans, and her denim colored shirt was tucked into her pants. Michael was used to seeing her in a baseball cap, but now her head was uncovered and her dark brown hair was parted and damp where it curled around her collar.

Laura knocked on the front door and then opened it, and Michael plopped down on the sofa as if he'd been caught doing something he shouldn't have been doing.

"Little man," Laura said, smiling, closing the door behind him. "What's going on?"

Michael shrugged his shoulders.

"Nothing," he said.

Laura put her hands on her hips and stood there looking around the living room, and then she looked at Michael.

"Where's your mom at?"

"She's in the bathroom," he said. "Getting ready."

Laura nodded her head, and then she turned and hollered down the short hallway that led to the bedrooms. "Hey, Jodi," she said. "I'm here."

"Come on back," Michael's mother said. "I'm getting ready, but y'all can leave whenever you want to."

Michael watched Laura climb down from her truck and start up the short sidewalk to the house.

Laura looked back at Michael and smiled, and then she turned and walked down the hallway. "You ain't getting rid of me that easy, Jolene," she said.

Michael heard his mother laugh, and then he heard the bedroom door close.

■ ■ ■

"You had any lunch yet?" Laura asked. They'd pulled off Michael's street, and they were cruising down Highway 150 toward downtown Shelby.

"No," Michael said.

"You hungry?"

"I guess."

"Which one you like better?" Laura asked. "McDonald's or Bojangles'?"

"McDonald's has a Playland," Michael said.

Laura drove in silence for a moment like Michael had given the wrong answer. Bright green trees flashed by outside her window, and Michael turned his head and saw open farmland spreading itself out on his side.

"So, that's the one you want?" Laura finally said. "McDonald's?"

"If I can play," Michael said.

■ ■ ■

After they ate lunch in near-silence, Michael climbed behind the mesh netting that separated Playland from the rest of the outdoor dining area. He waded, thigh deep, through plastic balls on his way to a rope ladder that led to a bridge connecting two towers. He wondered if Laura was watching him, and when he turned he saw that she was lighting a cigarette and watching Michael over the lighter's flame. She put the lighter in her pocket and narrowed her eyes and waved, the cigarette dangling from her mouth. Michael waved back before climbing the rope ladder as fast as he could.

For the next half hour or so, Michael took the rope ladder up into the first tower, took the bridge across to the second, and then took the corkscrew slide back down to the pool of plastic balls. After awhile he just sat in the balls with nothing but his face and maybe his ears visible, and he watched other kids do the same things he'd been doing. He imagined that he looked like a frog whose face had just broken the surface of a pond. At one point, when no one was coming, he even leapt from the balls like a frog would, and then he nestled himself back into them again.

He closed his eyes like he'd seen frogs in cartoons close theirs, and once he did he understood why they do it; he could hear everything: the rumble of the cars and trucks passing by in front of McDonald's; the pounding footsteps of the other kids as they ran from one tower to the other across the bridge above him; the voices of an adult couple in the picnic area whose kids must've been playing.

Then he heard Laura on her cell phone again. "Well he'd better step on it, Charlie," she said. "This is our big debut, and the thing's scheduled to happen at 2:00, and I can promise you that crane operator ain't going to wait too long after that."

Michael opened his eyes and saw that a girl about his age had climbed inside the ball pit, and she was hunkered down in the balls like he was and staring at him.

"Were you asleep?" she asked.

"No."

"Then why were your eyes closed?"

"Because I was pretending to be a frog," he said.

"Frogs have eyes."

"I know."

"Is that your mom?" she asked. She was looking through the mesh toward one of the picnic tables behind Michael.

"No," Michael said.

■ ■ ■

A steady stream of adults, most of them men in blue jeans and work boots, walked past the windows on either side of Laura's truck where they waited in traffic; Michael didn't see any kids. He'd known something was wrong as soon as Laura had lined up behind other cars and trucks waiting to get into the fairgrounds. He wanted to say something about it, but he didn't quite know what it meant to see all those adults, and he didn't know how he'd say it even if he did. But as soon as they crested the hill before turning into the gravel parking area, Michael knew what he'd felt a few minutes ago had been right: the fair was gone. There was no Ferris wheel peeking out above the fence that surrounded the grounds, and there were no tracks that belonged to the rickety roller coaster he'd refused to ride with his mother. There was nothing.

He wanted to look over at Laura, but he was afraid he might cry if he did.

"Where's the fair?" he finally asked.

"The fair?"

"I thought we were going to the fair."

"We are, kind of," Laura said. "We're going to a home show, which is a little bit like a fair."

There was no Ferris wheel peeking out above the fence that surrounded the grounds, and there were no tracks that belonged to the rickety roller coaster he'd refused to ride with his mother.

"How?" Michael asked. He looked over as Laura honked her horn at the truck in front of them.

"There's food and candy," she said. "And they'll have free T-shirts and hats. They'll be giving all kind of stuff away."

"Are there any rides?"

"No," she said. "No rides."

"Are the animals still here?"

"Nope," she said. "No animals either."

Laura looked over at Michael as if it were just becoming apparent to her that he was disappointed.

"But I've got something cool to show you later," she said. "I think you're going to love it. I promise."

Laura parked the truck, and Michael unfastened his seatbelt and climbed out and closed the door. The gravel lot was almost full of cars and trucks and people, and around the perimeter of the lot sat dozens of new modular homes: one-story homes like the house he and his mother lived in and larger two-story homes that had attached garages. Without yards or driveways, the houses seemed marooned out in the sun and heat. People waited in line to go inside the houses. Through the windows, Michael could see them wandering around the rooms.

Laura had lit a cigarette and was already walking across the parking lot toward the long, silver-colored agricultural halls, the same buildings that had housed the livestock at the fair. Michael ran and caught up with her.

"This is where me and Mom saw all the animals," Michael said.

"Yeah?" Laura said. "You like animals?"

"Yes."

"I got a buddy down in Anderson who's got an orangutan named Robby," she said. "He's an ornery old thing. The monkey, not my buddy."

"Does he work at a zoo?" Michael asked.

"No," she said. "He's just got this monkey who's been living with him for about ten years. He keeps him in a big cage out in the side-yard. He's got him a trampoline in there so he can bounce around all he wants to." Laura smiled and looked down at Michael. "Would you like to see that? A monkey on a trampoline?"

"Yes," said Michael, smiling.

"Okay," she said. "I'll call my buddy and we'll all go down there sometime: me, you, and your mom."

The three largest buildings were laid out end-to-end in a line that ran alongside the boundary to the fairgrounds. When Michael followed Laura into the first building he saw that it was dusty and dimly lit by overheard lights, just like it had been during the fair, but instead of livestock and cattle, the building was full of a dozen shining eighteen-wheelers, their hoods up and their doors open, people standing on ladders and looking down into the engine compartments, others sitting in passenger seats or exploring sleeping areas in the cabins. Each of the trucks was hitched to a trailer that held a segment of a one-story modular home. Men and women in nice clothes stood by sets of stairs leading up to each trailer, handing out folders and answering questions.

"Let's check out a couple of these while we wait," Laura said.

"What are we waiting for?" Michael asked.

"You'll see."

They walked toward a man in a suit who started talking, telling them about the home they were about to go into, but Laura just smiled and nodded at him and went right past him without saying anything. Michael followed him up the steps, through a front door, and into a foyer.

Once they were inside, Laura turned and looked at Michael.

"When you say 'home,' a lot of people only think about those old-timey brick houses, or maybe they picture one of those old white two-stories with wood siding." She reached out and rubbed her open palm across the wall inside the front door. "But all that's changing," she said. She turned and looked at Michael. "Now, you tell me if this house looks any different on the inside than any place your friends live in."

Michael could've told Laura that he didn't really have any friends, not yet anyway, at least not since they'd moved to Shelby and he'd started the second grade. But instead he looked around and understood what Laura meant; inside it looked just like any other foyer in any other home. On either side of him and Laura were entrances to rooms, and Michael imagined that one would eventually be used as a dining room and the other as a den. The only thing that seemed out of the ordinary was the sheet of heavy, white plastic that served as a partition and ran the length of the trailer. The plastic stirred slightly as if there were a breeze blowing through the foyer.

"Did you know the house you live in is a modular home?" Laura asked.

"No," Michael said.

"It's true," Laura said. "I know it for a fact because I helped put it up."

A few minutes later and two trailers over, Michael and Laura were making their way through a crowded kitchen and toward a backdoor off a laundry room when Laura made eye contact with a woman whose face seemed to say she knew her. "Shit," Laura whispered.

The woman was about Michael's mother's age, pretty with wavy brown hair and dark eyes. She wore jeans and a white button-down shirt that she'd left untucked. She had on lace-up work boots like Laura's. "Well, well, well," she said, looking at Laura first, and then at Michael.

"Hey, Charlotte," Laura said. She put one hand in her pocket and the other one around Michael's shoulders. It was the first time Michael could remember Laura touching him, and he stepped closer to her, and then he leaned his shoulder into her.

"Who's this?" Charlotte asked.

"This is Michael," she said. "Jodi's boy."

Charlotte crossed her arms and stared at Michael as if she were waiting for him to admit to doing something wrong. "Okay," she finally said.

Michael felt Laura's arm leave his shoulders, and Michael leaned away from her.

"How you been?" Laura asked.

Charlotte looked from Michael to Laura, her arms still folded. "I'm good," she said. "Looks like you're doing fine."

"Yeah," Laura said. "I am." Laura grew quiet, and then she looked down at Michael before looking back up at Charlotte. "Well," she said, "it's good to see you. Tell Joseph I said hey."

"I will," she said. "You tell Jolene I said hey too."

"Who was that woman?" Michael asked. He'd followed Laura out of the agricultural hall, and they were back out in the sunlight, moving with crowds of people toward a corner of the parking lot, past all of the displayed homes.

"She's just somebody I used to know," Laura said. She stopped walking and turned around and looked at Michael. "And your mom doesn't need to know we saw her today, okay?"

"Okay," Michael said.

"I'm serious," Laura said. "It'll just worry her. Your mom's got enough going on."

"Okay," Michael said again.

Michael and Laura stopped walking once they reached an area that had been cordoned off with sawhorses and yellow construction tape. Hundreds of people stood all around them, all of them talking and pointing to the two identical homes that sat fifty yards away on the other side of the tape. The homes were resting atop steel girders, and steel cables ran up from the girders to two cranes that were parked on either side of the houses.

Laura nodded toward the cranes and looked down at Michael. "Remember earlier when I told you that there wasn't no difference between old-timey houses and modulars?" Michael nodded. "Well, there's one big difference," Laura said, "and you're about to find out what it is."

"All right, all right," a man's voice said. Michael thought he recognized it—both the voice and the phrase—and he looked around and saw two men standing on the running board of the crane on his left; one of them was a tall bearded man in a baseball hat. The man's hat said 97.9 FM: The Earthquake. Michael knew it was Ol' Boy Rodney, who his mother listened to on the radio every morning while she drove Michael to school.

"How y'all doing this afternoon?" Ol' Boy Rodney yelled.

The crowd responded with applause and cheers. The man who'd been standing beside Rodney hopped down and walked toward the crowd and ducked under the yellow tape. He smiled at Laura and the two of them shook hands.

"Looks like Ol' Boy made it," Laura said.

"Just barely," the man said. "I gave him what you wrote out. He promised he'd stick to it."

Ol' Boy Rodney looked down at an index card in his hand, and then he looked back up at the audience and shouted into the bullhorn. "I want to welcome y'all to the tenth annual Cleveland County Manufactured Home Show," he said. People cheered again. "And, as y'all know, this is the last day of the show, so we thought we'd send y'all off with a bang." He looked down at the index cards again and shuffled them. He gestured toward the two homes to his left. "Now, y'all might think these two beautiful homes over there are the exact same, and from the outside they are, all the way down to the glass missing in the windows. But don't judge a book by its cover.

"This home right here," he said, pointing to the house closest to him, "it was stick-built right on-site. For the past two weeks folks have been out here building this thing, and it's just beautiful, isn't it?" The crowd booed, and Ol' Boy Rodney laughed. "But this other house, well, it ain't nothing but a modular home made to look like a real house. It was brought in this morning on trailers and put together by Moss Lake Custom Homes just a few hours before the show opened." The crowd cheered and Laura clapped and put his fingers in her mouth and whistled. Ol' Boy Rodney waited a few seconds before saying anything else. "So, are y'all saying this modular is just as good as this here stick-built? Just as well put together? Just as sturdy?" The crowd roared again. "Well, we'll see about that. Go ahead, boys!" He pounded his fist on the door to the crane, and then he jumped down from the running board and disappeared in the crowd.

The crane's engine groaned to life in a dull, throaty vibration that Michael felt in his chest, and then he heard the engine on the other crane do the same. But soon he ignored the noise because he was watching the stick-built house being lifted slowly from the ground: ten feet, fifteen, and then twenty. It hovered there for a second, the crowd chanting "Drop it! Drop it!" And then it came down.

Michael had never seen anything like it in his life, and even at eight-years-old he knew it was something he'd never forget. The entire first floor of the house crumbled as soon as the steel girders hit the ground, the wood siding cracking in loud pops

The crane's engine groaned to life in a dull, throaty vibration that Michael felt in his chest...

that sounded like gunshots. Beams protruded through the roof at crazy angles, and the window frames on the second floor popped loose from the walls.

The second crane began to lift the modular home, but when it was dropped nothing really happened: a few pieces of the siding popped loose, but the roof didn't buckle. Once the crowd quieted down, a man in a hardhat climbed up on the girders of the modular home and scrambled onto the porch. He reached out and tugged on the door until it came open, and then he disappeared inside. A minute or two later he forced open an undamaged upstairs window and waved at everyone, and soon he came back out the front door and gave the audience a thumbs up.

"How about that," Ol' Boy Rodney said into the bullhorn.

Laura turned to the man who'd hopped down from the crane, and the two of them shook hands again.

■ ■ ■

Once Michael and Laura had left the fairgrounds and were passing the mall, just about to turn west onto Highway 74, Michael looked at Laura. "Who's Joseph?" he asked.

Laura sighed like she didn't want to give an answer, and Michael wished he hadn't asked it, but he didn't know what else to do, so he waited.

"Why are you asking me that?" Laura finally said.

"You told that woman Charlotte to tell him you said hey."

Laura rolled her window up as if the air rushing past her ear made it hard for her to hear. She drove in silence for a second.

"He's Charlotte's son," Laura said.

"How old is he?"

"He's ten," Laura said.

Michael looked out the window for a second, and then he looked at Laura. "What's he like?"

Laura came to a stop at the stoplight in front of the entrance to Wal-Mart. She and Michael watched cars pass in front of them. The light turned green, and Laura put her foot on the gas.

"He's okay," Laura finally said. "But you're better."

On the way back down his street, Michael looked out his window and noticed that the houses in his neighborhood all looked the same. The only differences were the colors and some of them had front porches and some of them didn't. A few had two-car garages that had been added on.

"Oh, Lord," Laura said when they pulled into Michael's driveway. Michael's mother was walking slowly up the sidewalk toward the house, holding onto her mother's arm. Grandma wore dark blue sweatpants, a white blouse, and black slip-on shoes. Her silver hair stuck up in the back as if she'd just gotten out of bed. Neither she nor Michael's mother had turned to look at the truck when Laura pulled in.

Laura shut off the engine and climbed out of the truck and left the door open. Michael sat and watched as Laura took his grandmother's other arm, and he and Michael's mother helped her up the porch steps, one at a time. The trees were just beginning to turn green again, and through the new leaves Michael saw the old barn leaning warily away from the house. It was far away and the foliage had started to thicken, but he could see the old, rotted wood and the rusted harvester parked alongside the barn in the late afternoon sun.

He watched as Laura took the keys from Michael's mother and unlocked the front door and opened it. Then Laura went back and took the old woman's arm again. "One more step," Laura said. And then they were all inside.

But Michael sat out in the truck a moment longer, the cab warm with the sun coming through the windshield. He stared at his house and tried to picture it lifted up off the ground by a huge crane or jacked up on a flat-bed trailer and delivered to its present location in its separate pieces. But he couldn't imagine his home that way. To look at it now was to see something finished, to witness something that seemed complete. ■

REFRAIN

The birches dizzy me, shaking down
their mint and white confetti crowns around
the Scarlet Tanager, a trilling sky-high king:

red come orange, come black, come green.

From this forest freshed with song,
a goose lay drawn, opened
in a field ringed in feathers—

orange come red, come black, come green.

The coyote cast a wing
and three coronets
back to feign molting,

a confetti whorled white come red, come green.

SANDRA MARCHETTI

SHADOW

Across clearings, an eye—Ted Hughes, "The Thought-Fox"

Mushrooms on the trail indicate
you haven't roved this prairie of late;

soft-sponged and pink, they're sweet
as the berries ripped in your teeth.

"Foxes are opportunistic feeders,"
notes a sign—I never mind

the goldfinches who arc my breeze
and swap big bluestem for trees

patiently trilling each leaf, those
last full masts of September.

Zig-zagged grass ripples from a felled
trunk, sunk in its thatch to rot.

Past piles of branches spoiled
to mash, a flaxen hay

wherein I catch your gleam—
spun gold you are a long-bodied

beam, slinking past imagined
houses down to the stream.

Hidden to your scruff in the gathering
dusk, I hold and release your stare,

that of a silver-eyed murderer
who smells breath in the air.

SANDRA MARCHETTI

WALKING

HEIDI SIEGRIST

Huntsville, Alabama

The Natural Well is a pit cave hidden in Monte Sano State Park, at the very northern tip of Alabama. At the end of a path under arching oaks weaving tunnels of leaves, you'll find an unmarked well with its walls crumbling and only a wire fence surrounding to keep adventurers from tumbling in. The cave is just a mouth in the ground, so deep that when you drop in a rock, you don't hear the echo of its landing for seconds. Throwing things into the well—rocks, acorns, a stick—was hypnotizing for me as a kid. Every time, I thought maybe I would never hear it land at all. Maybe it would take a route I couldn't see or imagine down there in the darkness.

I grew up at the foothills of the Appalachians. Technically, at least. A small, idyllic mountain reaching out toward further, wilder mountains from its spot in Huntsville, a good-sized Southern city. Monte Sano—Mountain of Health. In the late 1800s, a health resort opened at the top of the mountain so that wealthy patrons from all over the South could visit to recover their vitality from the crisp mountain air and mineral spring water. The resort fell into disrepair, but homes began to pop up at the edges of the 2000-acre state park. Even now, Monte Sano is a neighborhood whose inhabitants tend to be the kind of people who believe that hiking in the woods is as powerful as any antibiotic or therapy. At potlucks and PTA meetings, they give one another knowing looks to this effect. This mutually-agreed-upon magic always produced a sort of restlessness in me. I thought that health was what allowed you to launch forward with the greatest energy; a health resort, if you never left, was only as good as a beautiful prison, a pleasant death.

Still, I understood why people never wanted to leave the mountain. I felt it too. On summer evenings growing up, I could hear my neighbor playing the banjo on his porch. If I ventured further into the park, I could find teenagers—usually the same ones who worked as lifeguards at the local pool—smoking weed in the woods, wearing wool ponchos. Life on the mountain felt to me like one long, drawn-out autumn evening on a porch swing. A neighborhood of thinkers, observers, artists. Everyone on Monte Sano believes that Monte Sano is special, and that everyone born and raised there, no matter how far afield they venture, will be pulled back by the magnetism of the mountain.

In high school, I was sure of my plans to leave the South and never come back. I thought of Monte Sano as an unfortunate casualty of a necessary exodus. I wanted out of the endless suburbs of churchgoers, the billboards celebrating the same good-ol'-boy politicians, football as religion, and the kind of Southern pride that kept Confederate flag stickers lodged firmly on mud-stained pickup trucks. Almost everyone I knew came from families who had gone to the same schools and worked in the same family businesses for generations. Many of them had never left the South at all. That terrified me, the idea of staying in one place, frozen in a world that stayed the same around me. Anyone who was sure I would one day return, to Monte Sano or anywhere else below the Mason-Dixon line, was someone I wanted to prove wrong.

In the eighteen years I lived on the mountain, my favorite thing to do was to go for long walks and imagine all the different places I might one day explore. I walked in the middle of hilly, quiet streets, wondering about Spain, and jumped into ditches when cars came around the corner. I walked in the fog on fall mornings and in the wet summer dark, fantasizing about Seattle. Over and over again, miles through streets and trails I had seen my entire life. My pace would slow or quicken as I made plans to grow confidently into a non-Southerner.

One summer morning, I walked in the state park before it was hot enough for the bees to wake and buzz like angry water around the fountains at the park's entrance. The dirt under my feet, striped by sun, felt like a challenge only I was capable of rising to. Walk. Ahead were blue-green mountains throwing off imposing shadows that stretched out over two paths before me: one, toward dribbling waterfalls, and the other, into the woods. I took the one into the woods. The trail marker paint had faded almost completely from the trees, and I pretended it wasn't there at all—that I knew completely each path I ventured onto, in the blood coursing through my sneakered feet. But the birds seemed to mock me in the woods, like they knew that despite my fantasies, I didn't really belong here in the way I wanted to, as sure-footed as a lengthening shadow, or water running through the veins of a leaf.

The squirrels weren't so critical. They chased each other up and down the trees, fussing. Their voices, barking and excited, echoed upward as they attempted to best each other in some secret and endlessly entertaining game. They corkscrewed up the trunk, sending bark flying to the ground, and then ran back down. I could have watched a separate set of squirrels doing the same thing in each tree as I walked, and if I couldn't then claim my own voice in the woods, I was for the moment content to be their silent observer.

Chicago, Illinois

My college friends were delighted to have a friend from Alabama. They made jokes about bare feet and banjos, and I laughed along with them like I would never go back. In the winters, people invariably shook their heads at me and said, "This must be rough for YOU, huh! Have you ever seen snow in Alabama?"

Actually, I've seen plenty of snow on Monte Sano. They close off the big road down the mountain so that kids can spend the day sledding while their parents watch and drink beers around a bonfire at the edge of the woods. After you've sled down, it takes half an hour to walk back up. In Chicago, the winters are more confining, more harsh, but beautiful. I could sit in my dorm with a book, looking out over the snow-blanketed campus and listening to the yowling wind. Warm and safe and still, I began to forget about exploring.

College was an exercise in theoretical thinking, so much so that I began to wonder if I wasn't only a pathetically half-formed theory myself. In small classes, we read the great books and lived collectively an eighteen-year-old's daydream of truth and love and meaning, of building a better world. I spoke in class, but tended to frustrate myself. I could never quite get out what I wanted to say. Halfway through a sentence, I would lose my path to a full idea.

In theory, we were all leading important adventures through a hundred new ideas, but in reality I didn't do anything much except for read, drink, and walk. You could argue, in a lazily researched undergrad sociology paper, that walking is the most ancient ritual of solitude. Independence in unassisted and undirected movement. Prayer in repetition. Joy in motion.

I saw the water grand and frozen, hugely silent in January, and I saw it screaming with swimmers and littered with beer cans in June.

Usually I would walk to the Point, a park jutting out along the rocky shores of Lake Michigan along the Chicago Lakefront Trail. To get there, it was necessary to maneuver past students heading to the library and restaurants near campus, but the park itself could be counted on to appear vast and quiet.

I walked along the Point for four years and never knew it at all. The Lakefront Trail stretches twenty miles through the city, and I usually walked no more than three of these. Even in that small stretch, the lakefront was constantly changing, giving me the same feeling that classes did of being joltingly lost. I saw the water grand and frozen, hugely silent in January, and I saw it screaming with swimmers and littered with beer cans in June. I saw dog walkers and wedding photo shoots and days when the trail was so abandoned that all you could hear was waves hitting rocks. Instead of exploring the city, I resigned myself to its unknowability.

In Chicago, I learned to worry about walking alone. As students, we were fed cautionary tales that made me look to Lake Michigan as something that could never envelop me fully, as considerate of my safety as the Monte Sano trees were of their squirrels. People had been mugged or attacked along the trail. Catcalling was to be expected of old men on benches, and was the least possible evil. According to the safety seminar we had been required to attend the first week of college, I should have been committed to staying aware of my surroundings at all times. Chicago's South Side was dangerous, after all. So I turned my music down a little bit when I went out walking, enough to hear the pad of footsteps behind me. I adopted a posture that was hunched and hurried, and looked straight ahead instead of up at the trees. There was more to see at eye level anyway. The curve of the path ahead with its encouraging mile markers, the focused joggers with their panting dogs, the occasional loners who swayed and laughed to themselves. And of course, the lake, gorgeous with a mean streak, too big for the imagination, and always freezing cold.

Easter morning of my third year of college, I woke up wanting to run to the Point. It was the morning after my twenty-first birthday party. I had bought alcohol for the first time—Tennessee Honey bourbon. The morning was so foggy that I could only see where lake met sky by the slow lapping of waves against the horizon. I sat down on the rocks, facing the water where I couldn't see the city skyline, so that it was easy to imagine myself as a traveler in an abandoned land, waiting for a ship. I could almost see it bobbing, a dot in the distance directed by invisible but infallible coordinates. The wind stung my hands and flicked water onto my face.

I felt a little foolish, somehow, for coming here instead of sleeping late in my warm bed. A duck emerged from behind a rock, looking satisfied in the wet fog. Every few minutes he would bristle his little body so his tail wagged in time with the water, then he floated toward me with his beak up as if giving me permission to sit next to him on the shore. He looked so perfectly at home that the fog itself seemed to be radiating off of him. Imagine my life, he seemed to be saying. Imagine diving under this water with perfect confidence, perfect fearlessness, and coming up with a fish, never even questioning your movements.

Damascus, Virginia

My last autumn of college, I left Chicago to join my parents on a weekend trip to bike the Virginia Creeper Trail, a thirty-five-mile ride through gentle hills, farmland, and the thick woods of the George Washington and Jefferson National Forests. Guidebooks say the Virginia Creeper Trail is Just Lovely in the fall, and they're right. We flew past changing leaves, waterfalls, and quiet homes. At one point, the bike road crosses the Appalachian Trail, and you get a quick glance of its guidepost—a beckoning "A" shaped to curve upward like a pine tree.

The bike path ends in Damascus, a small town just along the Appalachian Trail. Each spring, Damascus hosts the Trail Days Festival, a weekend of parades, music, and food that brings more Appalachian Trail hikers together than at any other time or place. Damascus is home to only 800 people, but it is vibrant with welcoming travelers. Halfway down the Creeper Trail, we stopped at a little café at the edge of the woods—the only place along the route to eat or rest—and were ushered in with exuberant come-on-in-y'alls. The cafe offered a pleasantly limited menu: grilled cheese sandwiches on Wonder Bread, sweet tomato soup, and hot coffee in Styrofoam cups.

Right by the ordering window was a full-sized map, dotted all over with thumbtacks representing the homes of visitors who had biked the Creeper Trail. The tacks clustered into a forest, covering nearly every state in the U.S. Nearly every continent, in fact. London, Beijing, Sydney. They have all made the Trail deeper and more obvious, through each plot of grass and across every worn-down little bridge. Maybe they, like me, reached out to catch a leaf that fell at the perfect speed to intersect with their bicycles. Maybe they sat at this same picnic table, eating this same grilled cheese sandwich dunked in soup. Sitting there, I still felt the rush of the Trail under me, like the first few rhythmic moments after stepping off a boat. The ghost of togetherness.

We finished the Trail in the late afternoon, when the autumn light was just beginning to lose its energy. After returning our rented bikes, we found our way to a dark and languishing restaurant. I felt happiness as a pang in my chest, without knowing why. Maybe it was the return to the woods after so much time in the city, or the sight of my parents laughing on their bikes, or an unexpected love for this strange, tiny town. At the restaurant, we were presented with limp shrimp cocktails, half-warmed French onion soup, and beer. The bar advertised live music every night, and tonight the main act was a band of three kids around my age: "The Stragglers."

Like so many passers-through Damascus, they were walking the Appalachian Trail, and had ventured back into civilization to play a few songs and earn enough money for a round of drinks before heading back into the woods. They were true to their name, with dirty dreadlocks and knives hanging from mud-stained cargo pants, clearly not caring how they looked or smelled. They started their set without a word. Quick banjo, defiant fiddle, wistful guitar. The girl's voice was harsh and urgent, and her song seemed to be written in an ancient language of the Trail. If I could understand, I thought, I'd probably lose my mind or understand love or know how to roast a rabbit over an open fire. I felt, for the first time, that I could be of the South and in the South, but not the South wholly—not a frozen figure in a tourist's snow globe of Alabama.

It was incomprehensible to me how they had gotten the bravery to do what they were doing—walking, and just that. How long had they been traveling? Where did they come from, why did they leave, and where were they stopping next? What had they discovered? I couldn't even get up the nerve to ask. They seemed far away from me and everyone else sitting awed at the tables, picking at their shrimp cocktails.

In that restaurant in Damascus, the Appalachians planted themselves as part of my identity in the valleys of my brain. Stretching from Alabama to Maine, the mountains became an endless line of Monte Sanos. Folk musicians, artists, and environmentalists. Long stretches of wilderness, energetic and ruthless. I thought that to travel these mountains would be like journeying through a thousand of my own homes, each in a parallel universe where I, having sought out one of a thousand possibilities of my life, would meet a thousand different versions of myself.

For the next two years, I would think of The Stragglers whenever I was bored in Chicago, restless at my desk at work and wondering where I might go and what I might do to somehow arrive at a meaningful life. I hated sitting in the same place for eight hours a day, constructing unconvincing theories about the purpose of my work. A year after graduating college, I started considering quitting my job and taking to the Appalachian Trail, alone. I thought I would do it in May. Research, though, revealed it to be more complicated than my romantic fantasies. I would need long clothing, regardless of the heat, to protect against ticks and snake bites. I would also need camping gear and food, and at night, a rope to hoist my food up into the trees so that bears couldn't reach it. I was dismayed to realize that I would have too much to carry to bring along my banjo, bought impetuously in a fantasy of learning bluegrass music on the Trail, inspired by the breeze in the pines.

New Orleans, Louisiana

I ended up quitting my job in November, half a year ahead of my plan, to go to New Orleans for no good reason. Ruth, my best friend from high school and another Alabama expatriate, had suggested a Southern road trip that I was all too quick to agree to. Buying a banjo had spurred in me a string of uncharacteristically spontaneous decisions. I was learning that I was unbelievably free, as long as I was willing to bet everything I had acquired and saved on half-baked plans I thought might give me some idea of how to live.

After a week on the road, stopping in Kentucky and Tennessee to drink bourbon and eat barbecue, we found ourselves in the Big Easy, staying with Ruth's brother.

I liked the way the streets looked in New Orleans, colorful and busy. The effects of Hurricane Katrina had driven down the prices of property, and the city was beginning to see an influx of young artists and entrepreneurs from all over the country. People were coming here to become what they had daydreamed about becoming, and it was clear why. New Orleans possesses a magic that gives people an instinct for creating something beautiful out of all the disparate places they've belonged to. Franco-Spanish architecture, Cajun food, an unusual and dignified dialect that rejects certain "Rs". We were happy tourists. Roaming Jackson Square, we listened to jazz and studied paintings of cats eating beignets. For four days, I was drunk on cheap beer and the confidence of having arrived at some sort of destination.

We spent our last evening on Frenchmen Street in the Seventh Ward, where people weaved around sloshing drinks onto the cold sidewalk. Ruth's brother had recommended the area, scoffing at the kitsch of Bourbon Street. Frenchmen, he said, was where we would find Authentic New Orleans. Good music, good food, and the good sense of the locals—no touristy brawling. The street was a pulsing line in a grid of sleeping houses extending into distant palm trees and black sky. Left mostly untouched by Katrina and thereafter designated an official "Arts and Entertainment" district, Frenchmen gave off a fresh, surprised sort of joie de vivre. We sat in a dimly lit bar, listening to a jazz band made up of four middle-aged men in collared shirts. I didn't know enough about jazz to know if it was good, but it sounded playful and cynical, a little sad. Groups waiting to be called for dinner leaned against the dirty windows, watching the band, were thinking about their lives. You could see a woman move her lips slightly, imagining conversations, and a man close his eyes and sway like someone he loved was watching him enjoy the music.

I wanted to smell jambalaya on the street and walk by people offering to tell me my future.

After days on the road, New Orleans felt shockingly populated. I had come here for the most vague reasons I had ever gone anywhere in my life. I wanted to smell jambalaya on the street and walk by people offering to tell me my future. Just to see what I could see, feel what I could feel. Universe, what do you have for me? Everyone in the bar was asking the Universe the same question, and it was clear that the lines were tied up. My hands were sticky from jostled whiskey-Coke, and I was impatient. Watching the passersby outside stumble and laugh, I wondered if they knew where they were going. *Were they locals? What did that mean, exactly?* I wanted to run out and join them, beg them to play a drunken game of hide-and-seek with me in the darkest streets of the city.

Huntsville, Alabama

After New Orleans, Ruth dropped me off in Huntsville, and I spent a week back in Alabama with my mom. Maybe because of the nurturing wisdom of the Monte Sano air she loves, my mom is a strong believer in the perfect and unseen intricacies of our roads to intertwined fates. Each of these fates, she believes, is ultimately good and valuable to the world. Each of these fates will find us and lead us to where we are meant to be. This philosophy has made her kind and fearless. Like I was six-years-old again, I woke up early every morning and made my way to her bedroom, where coffee was already brewing and the cat was glaring at me for infringing on her territory.

Most days we sat in bed for an hour, watching the light change from the window. The trees were by now bare of leaves, and the garden grey. Bird feeders hung against the window, and cardinals and finches flapped up and settled a few feet away from us, pecking with singular ambition at the suet. The cat sat on the edge of the bed and whined at them, an urgent, sad sound of fruitless anticipation.

I walked every day of the week that I was home. Because I hadn't brought my sneakers, I wore my hiking boots, which were so worn through that they made my ankles bleed. Three miles, the same roads every day. Despite the aches in my feet, I couldn't help but feel the Monte Sano air expand and crackle with its mythical curative powers in my lungs. I rounded each corner with confidence, knowing exactly the lawn ornaments and the waving pines that would approach me at each block. Neighbors passed by, their dogs straining against leashes, and we all greeted each other, raising our voices above the breeze. In a few days, back in Chicago, my friends would ask me how my road trip was. I would say, great, it felt important to me. And I would leave it at that, not knowing what else to say. How do you express your gratitude for health, for luck, for the chance to roam?

Nowhere

The Appalachian Trail is traditionally walked from South to North, beginning at a peak in Georgia and ending at one in Maine. 2,200 miles of walking, the entire trail is completed by only one out of four of the "thru hikers" who attempt it, usually taking about six months. In that time, you are dwarfed by oaks, yellow poplars, birches, and evergreens. You learn to watch for black bears and copperheads—like any place, the Trail has its dangers. Facing the Appalachians is the ultimate proof of your dedication as a walker, a sign that you are meditative and brave, have seen the land and listened, and understood it well enough to be granted asylum within its walls. This asylum has always been necessary—the Trail was conceived in 1921 by a retired forester as a refuge from the confinements of modern life. Since then, modern life has barreled forward, but our Appalachian retreat from it has remained largely the same. Almost one hundred years of footsteps. The owners of those footsteps must feel linked to one another in some immeasurable way. A community you will never leave, or truly come home to.

These hikers have their homes, unmovable thumbtacks on a yellowing world map, and they have in their eyes and hands and ears and throats all the other places they've found themselves.

I always imagined that if I could walk the trail, I would go from North to South, starting out a stranger in Maine. But I wouldn't stop in Georgia. I would keep going down further, falling into smaller trails, until I found myself in woods I could recognize without a map—Monte Sano. Mountain of Health. I'd come home by the Natural Well Trail, stopping to drop in a rock and hear it land, a resounding joyful yelp, echoing up like my own voice. ■

NESTS

1.
Dad held our dog up high as his arms stretched,
by the scruff of her neck, a black-furred mar
against the summer sky. Mother wasn't home;
we saw him and hid in the folded-down pop-up camper,
its perfect skirt of weeds anchoring it to the yard.
The crawl space, when folded down, was large enough
for three girls to crawl inside. If you don't mind
the all-encompassing heat, and the wasps, hovering,
uncertain in the darkness, landing and flexing.
We closed the door behind us, and we held it closed.

2.
Every time I see a wasp, I take it as a warning.
I don't go where a wasp is. I don't open a door
that a wasp hovers outside of. My sister was chased
by a wasp, stung seven times in the back as she ran
for the house. I like to think I've never been stung
because I am very careful.

3.
I've never once been stung
though my two-year-old daughter
has now—on her ankle, clean
as an unpaid bill, a puncture
we coated with baking soda paste,
wrapped in cellophane.

Her grandfather, on my husband's side,
a surgeon, tied a bow around the bandage,
because she asked him to. Steve was careful
with the wound, careful in a way
that would have made my father laugh.

4.
Wasps built nests in the vents
of my childhood bedroom
every summer. Buzzing
in the vents, drifting down
through the slats. After
they were sprayed, I'd find
them in the mornings curling
and uncurling the deep red
bodies. Crisp-shelled, dark-winged.
Searching to sting, I thought
at the time, but now see it as
a display of pain.

RENEE EMERSON

HARD-TO-REACH BACKPARTS

HOLLY GODDARD JONES

I can't use a curling iron without thinking of my mother. As a girl I had stick-straight hair, and so for special occasions—Easter Sunday, kindergarten graduation, school pictures—Mom would sit me down on the living room floor between her knees, plug in the iron, and start giving me a look to equal the occasion. Even now, if you see me with curls, you'll know that I think the situation calls for a little something extra. Mornings like this one, I look at myself in the mirror and see a flash of that girl I was, even though my curled hair is spiked with grey and I have lines on my face.

I never curl the hard-to-reach back parts without wishing Mom could do it for me. What a soothing pleasure (occasionally punctuated with the surprise pain of a slip of the iron, so that it grazed the top of an ear or nape of the neck) to sit on a shag carpet in your bathrobe and have your mother's hands in your hair. Even that burning hair smell—even that. Bottle it and let me take a whiff whenever I'm stressed out. Her legs brushing my arms and some boring Sunday PBS show on the TV and the whole house smells like bacon. Her whispered count to thirty for each curl. ■

STALKING
THE WHITE DEER

NATALIE SYPOLT

Dalton stalked the white deer. It became his obsession, like finding that thing and owning it in a hard, bloody way would fill a hole neither of us could name. We were newly married then and him just back from the war. He'd been home about a year, but it always seemed like he was just back. For years. Even now. It was always lingering there, but our boys came back into their lives, all messed up—in body and in spirit—and went right back to it. Bury it in the mines. Cut it down with the trees. Drive, drink, drug, and screw it away. But don't name it.

I told him to leave the white deer be and he laughed at me. "Jezzie, girl, did you get all soft on me while I was gone? Do you want to make a pet out of that deer?" Some men liked gentle and sweet women, but the Crystal men wanted girls who could never be called delicate. Maybe it had to be that way because of the kind of life we live. Some fragile little thing would never survive it, would end up in a crazy house or in the ground.

First Dalton only wanted the white deer—he'd seen it once, out behind his daddy's house, and it had been so shocking that he'd blinked a few times to make sure that he wasn't looking at a dog or a ghost. "When it ran away," he told me, "it was like smoke or mist moving through the trees." He wanted it so bad that he wouldn't take any others, and I started to worry that we'd have no deer meat to put up for the winter. I didn't have long to worry, though, because then Dalton got bad and started killing all those deer just out of rage. Our little yard was full of deer, hanging from trees, dripping blood. He killed them faster than we could butcher them. They started rotting, and the smell turned to something different than just death.

Dalton stayed out every hour he could, roaming along the ridges with his gun, searching for that white deer.

My belly was big then. We thought there would be just one baby, but when I grew and grew, we went to the doctor over in Oakland and he said that there'd be two. I thought about what my granny used to tell me about twins, how the old folks thought it wasn't natural, and how some wouldn't let both babies live. "I ain't saying that's right," Granny said, "but I ain't never seen a set where both turn out good." Granny was old then, and her face was shriveled like a dried up apple, but she had these blue eyes that seemed almost to glow. I was only a girl, fourteen or fifteen, and she just stared right into me, like she knew one day I'd be sitting in this drafty old house, full to the brim with babies, dead animals rotting all around me.

When Dalton came in from the woods, he'd go back to the bedroom and strip off all his clothes, covered in blood and other dark stains that I couldn't think about. He'd shower quick and then come out into the kitchen, where I'd have his dinner—little that it was—waiting. He wouldn't put clothes back on, and I never could get used to seeing him walk around in the kitchen, pale and skinny, without a stitch on. It embarrassed me and I couldn't look at him straight on, like some little girl seeing a man for the first time. Sometimes, he'd think it was funny, and laugh that mean little laugh he had, then press up against me, just to feel me try to squirm away. Other times he'd look at me with disgust. "You act like the Virgin Mary," he'd say and sneer. "Well them ain't God's babies rolling around inside you."

"That's ugly talk," I'd say. He'd shrug and sit down at the table, eat his dinner with that blood and mud deep under his fingernails and in the creases of his knuckles.

Rabbits, groundhogs, raccoons, lying all around our little house. Then that red fox. It had started to snow and his bright coat stood out among all the others. I saw it from the kitchen window and had to go out, a part of me maybe hoping it was still alive and that Dalton wouldn't have killed such a beautiful thing just because he could, just because he couldn't have what he really wanted. His work coat was hanging by the door, and I wrapped it around me. I was so big then with the babies that it would barely stretch across. I liked the smell of it that reminded me of Dalton—the woods and the grease from the coal trucks he worked on for Shaffer's trucking.

More and more he'd been missing work, taking off all or part of the day to roam the ridges. They'd been understanding and old man Shaffer had grown up with Dalton's daddy, but I knew one day they'd have had enough and Dalton would have no job. Some nights, I'd look at his face as he leaned over his dinner plate, and I'd get so afraid of what I saw there. He could lose his job and not care a bit. Me and him and the babies could starve to death or freeze to death in the coldest days of winter, and still he would not care.

Dalton had tossed the fox next to the wood pile, already lower than it had been since we'd lived there. His eyes were open and as I got closer, I thought maybe he was still breathing. I am ashamed to say that then I started hoping and hoping that it was not so. I did not know how to take care of an injured fox. I did not want to try. The beautiful thing was dead, though, the tip of his tongue out the side of his mouth, the white scruff of his neck brown with dried blood.

Dalton was standing in our little kitchen when I came back inside. He had spent all morning since before dawn stalking that white deer, but must have come in from the ridge while I was out back with the fox. My stomach clenched, thinking about what new dead thing he'd soon have strung up in our

The beautiful thing was dead, though, the tip of his tongue out the side of his mouth, the white scruff of his neck brown with dried blood.

trees, but then I saw that his hands were clean, and so were his clothes. Nothing this morning.

"What were you doing, Jezzie?" he asked.

"I just went out to check the woodpile," I lied. "It's getting low." He came toward me then and though he'd never hit me, someplace inside I always knew that he could, that all men could. I took a step back, my hand stretching for the door handle, but when Dalton reached me, he wasn't angry.

He put his big hands on my cheeks and said, "Cold?" I nodded. He said, "Come over to the fire. Your feet—" My feet had been too swollen for weeks to put on my boots so I'd went out in my house slippers. The snow had collected around the tops. I hadn't even noticed.

Dalton led me to the big chair next to the fire and kneeled down in front of me. "What were you thinking, Jezzie girl? Your feet are like ice." He pulled the slippers off and began rubbing my freezing feet, blowing hot breath on my toes, and then kneading my skin with his strong hands.

"He is pushing life back into me," I thought, as the burning pain of feeling poured into my feet.

"I'm sorry, Jezzie," he said, so low I could barely hear him. When I felt his lips gently kiss the top of my burning foot, a jolt shot through me that nearly made me laugh and cry all at the same time. "I'll go cut more wood for the pile. Don't you worry about that."

"I ain't worried," I said. I wanted to reach down to him and cup his face in my hands, but my big belly stopped me.

"I'll go right now," he said, but instead kissed my ankle.

"No, don't go," I said, and stretched my hand out for him, though he was just out of my reach. Dalton rubbed my calf and kissed my knee, pushing my house dress up over my thighs. A young woman still and here I was wearing a house dress and slippers like a granny. Dalton kissed the inside of my thigh and I thought about the boy he had been, the tow-headed kid who sat behind me every year in school because my last name started with a B and his started with a C. The boy with a daddy so mean he'd sometimes cut Dalton's hair in an awful way to punish him for not doing something fast enough. He'd come to school with chunks taken out of the side—his scalp raw and pink underneath. I suppose his daddy was hoping to humiliate him, but the other kids were too scared of the Crystals to ever make fun.

Once, he'd saved a kitten whose mother got ran over on the county road. The kitten was so tiny, and he fed it with an eye-dropper until it got big enough to eat on its own.

Once, he gave me his lunch money because I didn't have any.

Once, he took my hand and led me out to the cemetery and showed me where all the generations of Crystals were buried. "We're all here," he'd said. "Planted right here in this ground while we're living and while we're dead." I knew he was telling me that he could never leave Warm, and if I wanted to be with him, I could never leave either.

He kissed the inside of my thigh and I remembered the girl I was, not some scared little mouse, shivering in a corner. I was a strong girl who chopped wood all those months Dalton was away, who worked at the five-and-ten in town and who hadn't been scared of much of anything.

"He is pushing life back into me," I thought again as he put his hands on either side of my belly. "I will do the same for him."

■ ■ ■

"Don't cut that wood," he said into my ear the next morning before leaving for work. I was at that place of fuzzy awakeness and at first thought he said, "Don't forget good."

"I won't," I mumbled, and he kissed my temple.

"I mean it," he said. "Don't chop the wood. I'll do it when I get home."

He was the old Dalton, the Dalton before he left Warm for the war and forgot how to stop killing, but I knew it wouldn't last. I'd seen it before—a day or even two or three of the boy I knew, but then the dark would come back into his face and he'd start seeing things in his head again that I couldn't understand.

I put on my heaviest sweater and found a pair of Dalton's pants in the closet. Nothing I had fit me anymore—only those old housedresses, and I knew this was not a job I could do in a dress. I put on three pairs of socks, then shoved my feet down into his old boots. They were still too big, but would have to do. I smiled to see that he'd left his work coat hanging on a hook by the door for me.

If I'd had a brother, my daddy's rifle would have gone to him, but since I didn't, it had been mine after he'd died. I kept it clean and oiled, but I hadn't shot it in years. I knew how, though, and that was one of those things that once you learned, you never did forget. When I put the butt up to my shoulder and looked through the sights, my finger curled around the trigger just like it had been waiting to do that for so long.

I thought about going back to Dalton's daddy's house where he'd first spotted the white deer, but that seemed too dangerous. His daddy or one of his brothers might have seen me. So I just started walking out of Crystal Holler, up Backbone Mountain. It was cold enough to see my breath, but not as cold as the day before. There was a dusting of new snow. If I got close to any animal, it'd be easy enough to see its tracks.

I can't explain how I knew where to go. I thought maybe God had led me there to find that white deer, to take her life and save my own. But now, as an old woman who has seen a life of one hard, heartbreaking thing after another, I can say that if there is a God, he is a son of a bitch, and if that day in the woods was a test, I failed it.

I'd been out for only an hour or so, trying to keep quiet as I could. I slipped once and went down to one knee. I'm ashamed to say that I did not stop then to think about my babies and what would happen to them if I tumbled down the steep hillside. Throughout my life, I have always thought more about my husband than those boys, and that is my great shame. That is what happens, though, when you love a boy from the time you were both children, when you can't stand to love anything more.

She stepped right out in front of me, maybe a hundred yards or so ahead of where I had stopped to catch my breath. It was just like Dalton had said, a ghost deer so white I wasn't sure she was real. She stopped when she saw me and just stood there, staring, steam from her nose floating out around her head.

What I should say is that she was so beautiful that I didn't want to kill her. The truth, though, is that as I raised the rifle to my shoulder and put the crosshairs on the white deer's neck, I could already see the red rose blooming through her coat, her falling to the ground.

"Good girl," I thought, but did not say. I did not want to spook her. I was a good shot, and I knew where I should hit the

She stepped right out in front of me, maybe a hundred yards or so ahead of where I had stopped to catch my breath.

deer to make it all quick and easy. I did not want to chase her through the woods, injured and frantic. I did not want her to suffer. A good hunter knows not to take a life for granted.

My finger squeezed the trigger and I barely felt the kick against my shoulder. Just as I imagined, the deer jerked and then fell. The blood, though, was not a bright red like I'd pictured. As I walked to her, I saw that it was dark, nearly black, and spread over her neck not like a rose, but like an ugly stain, spilled paint. She was not breathing or moving, and that at least was something.

I had not thought about what would happen next, how I would get the white deer down from the ridge, or if I should slit her belly there like I knew the men did. If you let it go too long, if you didn't stick them and bleed them, the meat will turn bad. I could not imagine eating the meat of the white deer, or frying it in a pan. I gagged at the thought.

I heard a rustling over in the bramble, and then a crying sound, a scream almost. A sickness came over me as the knowing set in. There shouldn't have been a baby now, not at this time of the year, but there it was, spindly legged and spotted. I now knew why she hadn't run from me, smart girl protecting her little one.

"Oh, I'm sorry," I said to the fawn. "I'm sorry, baby."

"Jezzie?" I started. In my craziness—my exhaustion—I thought the deer was saying my name. "What are you doing? What—"

Through the woods behind me came Dalton, carrying his own rifle. He hadn't gone to work at all like he'd said, but was up on the ridge, just like me. He looked from me to the white deer, and then to the bleating fawn in the brush. "Jesus Christ," he said. "What are you doing?"

"I just wanted to help you," I said. I made to touch his arm, but he pushed me away.

"Have you lost your fucking mind?"

"Dalton—"

"Go home," he said, staring down at the white deer.

"I can help. We can drag her out of here, and then this can be over," I said. I saw him look over at the fawn, still standing uncertainly in the brambles, wanting to go to its mother.

"Go home," Dalton said again. "Go now."

There was no use in arguing. Only more harm would come if I tried, so I turned and started carefully away from my kill. I wanted to believe that maybe Dalton would save that fawn, coax it over to him and wrap it up in his big arms, nurse it with a baby bottle like he did that kitten when he was a boy.

If he had done that, then I would have known this all could still be set right, and that our lives could take on a different shape—maybe a rose shape again, but I had only taken a few steps when I heard the crack of the rifle. For a crazy minute, I thought maybe Dalton had put the barrel of the rifle under his own chin. Lord knows it wouldn't have been the first time someone from around here'd had a hunting accident like that, but when I turned, I saw his back, shoulders slumped forward, crying.

■ ■ ■

Some folks think it's cowardly to kill a white deer because they're so easy to see with no natural camouflage. Others say it's bad luck. I don't believe in luck, but I do know this: when Dalton came down from the ridge that day, he did not bring the white deer or the fawn. He did borrow his father's tractor and dig a big hole. He spent two days hauling the dead animals into that hole, as I watched from the kitchen window. I couldn't get the sound of that baby crying out of my head, or stop picturing the way Dalton's shoulders shook after he killed it. Those were my burdens to carry, though, and I'd do it gladly if it meant my husband was fixed. What I did not know then, could not know, was that a human cannot be fixed. They can be patched, and soothed, and made to remember a little less, but fixed is something Dalton would never be.

When my babies came, they came early. Dalton drove me to the hospital in Oakland, his knuckles white where they clutched the steering wheel, and his lips a tight, thin line. He did not speak to me the whole drive, and stared only straight ahead.

Walker came into the world a screaming fire ball, but Sam was born quiet and with the caul covering his face. My granny would have shaken her head with worry, but she was long dead by that time. The doctor said what good luck it was, and rare, to see a baby born that way. The doctor said Sam would be blessed his whole life. I wondered what that meant for Walker, the baby who always cried.

I watched my boys grow, loved them the best I could and I truly think Dalton did the same, in the only ways he knew how. Sometimes that was a backhand to the mouth, other times it was an arm across the shoulder. He helped them with the hard things, like burying their dog when it got run over by the mailman, then burying their grandfather when an aneurysm burst in his brain. I cooked them dinner, and washed their clothes, and gave them dollars at the end of every week, even when there weren't many dollars to go around. I tried to help them be good boys—the both of them—and I tried not to notice the shining light around Sam, or the dark shadow around his brother. Sometimes I'd remember that white deer and the baby, screaming in the brush, and I'd punish myself by thinking, "Which one, Jezzie? If you could save just one baby, which one would it be?" On my most honest days, I knew it would be Sam, so I showered Walker with love. I made him special things for dinner, and snuck him an extra quarter or two when I could. Sam pretended never to notice or to care, because he was good in a way none of the rest of us was. He was a smart boy, and sweet. They both were so handsome. But they were Crystals, and even the good Crystals have a dark side that craves booze and drugs and driving fast and living hard. I knew this, always, and I chose it. Is killing the white deer what cursed my boys or was it marrying Dalton Crystal?

When Walker and Sam were fifteen, Dalton took them to the family cemetery and said to them, "This is your kin, boys, all of it. We're all planted right here in this ground while we're living and while we're dead." He was asking them to make the decision, just as he had me all those years ago. Are you going to be one of us?

Dalton and me, we are here, together, for better or worse in the life we deserve. If I had it to do over again, even after all that has happened, I suspect I would do it just the same way. When people look at us, living here in this holler with not much money or anything else, and say, "What's wrong with you?" I guess that's the answer. We stayed, we stay, we always will. Through ugliness, and blood, one boy dead and one tattered, we are our stain, the stain that we made. ■

FLIGHT

Our twelve-seater sits on concrete
cracked and filled with rubber
on a mountaintop just a hair shorter
than the bare ridge beside, already
ripped of leaves save the tough red oak
making a stand amongst grey poplar
and the broad green flanks of pine.

This planescape begins to move, spinning
the ball of your eye into a blur that can no
longer hold the shapes of all you know, love,
and are loathe to leave. The frog-green creek
is threading into its river, now, and before
that can vanish you start naming two-lanes
and hollers, holding on to cars and houses
even big mine trucks and slurry ponds,
which are tipping now, as the wings turn,
without draining.

Then the clouds. Then the letting go.
As we lift into blue the woman next to me
slackens into sleep, her elbow pressing
into the flesh of my forearm. It is soft.
She must need the sleep—at least
that is what I decide to say if questioned—
so for one hour and twenty minutes
I do not move, until the judder of down-flaps
untethers our touch, releasing us like two
balloons into our separate dreams
of things on earth. *Did I snore,* she says,
with a sheepish smile. *No,* I say, as if we

two are young lovers who still have secrets
we yearn—but cannot bear just yet—to tell.

BILL KING

HAWKS AT DUSK

for William Kirk

Tonight will be the longest night
in the history of the Earth, I am told,
but even such a little eternity beggars
imagination, while the things of this world,

illuminated by the distant sun, do not.
They still deserve our attention: twelve
red-tails on the way back from your memorial
today, one on the top of a steel light post

just outside Fairfax, one crossing in flight
low over the road, and the rest in the high
arms of trees along the two-lane that splits
the George Washington and the Thomas

Jefferson National Forests. You knew this area
well. Your childhood friend said you could walk
its rocky trails in the dark, so maybe you knew
what you were doing when you took your leave of us.

They will eat carrion, hawks, but more often
are the silent shadow that precedes mercy. They
carry the wounded skyward. Will, I do not know
what wildfire raged in your heart, what wind

outflanking the hard won line, blew up in your face,
but I'm sure you would have seen each one of them
while the rest of us, stuck in the traffic of our
crowded byways, would not. Let me tell you,

except for the one in flight, they were standing
at attention like tomb guards at the National Cemetery
who don their blue plumage in any weather,
and never forget.

BILL KING

AN *APPALACHIAN HERITAGE* INTERVIEW

WILEY CASH

Wiley Cash and I sit in the Rhododendron Lodge dining room at Virginia's Breaks Interstate Park, where he is the guest author for the Appalachian Writing Project's annual Writing Retreat. A wall of glass gives us a panorama of peaks and cliffs that are known as the "Grand Canyon of the South" and are shrouded by lush, July trees. The eye falls to the Russell Fork River gorge that divides these mountains, flanked by a railroad mostly hidden in the spring and summer months.

At just thirty-six, Cash is already the author of two bestselling novels, *A Land More Kind Than Home* and *This Dark Road to Mercy,* of which the latter has been optioned for film. The novels' dark plots are infused by two southern staples, religion and baseball, and both take an unflinching look these traditions from a child's point of view.

A summer storm is rolling in as we sit down. Thunder echoes through the valley and the building shudders. It seems a fitting backdrop as we begin by talking about *A Land More Kind Than Home.*

■ ■ ■

AMY CLARK: I read that this novel was based on a true story.

WILEY CASH: I was living in Louisiana, and I really missed the North Carolina mountains where I'd been living most of the time. I was taking a class in African-American literature, and we had just read James Baldwin's *Go Tell It on the Mountain.* We were talking about coming through narratives—how a character will have a religious conversion and come through and the theatrics of that—and our professor brought in a story out of Milwaukee about a young boy with autism in an African-American storefront church. They had tried to heal, by exorcising the "spirit" of autism from him, by laying hands on him and laying [their bodies] on him. They ended up crushing him. Obviously, it's tragic, but also interesting. I was interested in a group of believers who would take their convictions to that extent.

I didn't know anything about Milwaukee. I didn't know Louisiana well enough to set a story there, either, but I knew

I could put this in North Carolina. I figured it would be somewhere evangelical, somewhere charismatic. Probably a Holiness church that believed in laying of hands, speaking in tongues. I thought, well, if I'm going to write about it I need to find a place that would want to keep it secret, and Madison County, North Carolina, felt like that kind of place. I knew Madison pretty well. I'd lived around there for a long time. I knew that place is...kind of insular. If I could put this novel in the 1980s, this would have happened then.

[My] second book, which is about two little girls who were kidnapped by their father, a washed-up baseball player, was inspired by two stories. My wife told me a story about being a little girl and her dad teaching her how to slide into base on a softball field near her house. I just had a vision of a dad and his little girl on a baseball field. But it wasn't really a story...it's not complicated.

I remembered these two little girls who I grew up with in Gastonia. They were foster children being raised by an elderly couple in my church. When they went back to their birth mother, they ended up being murdered by these two guys they were dating. Those stories came together: baseball backdrop, fathers and daughters, two young girls in peril. That just started spinning out the potential in my mind.

I set *A Land More Kind Than Home* in the mountains of North Carolina because I missed the mountains, and I set the second novel in Gastonia because I grew up there. I knew that town and I knew those landmarks, what kind of family this would happen to.

AC: We see so much detail through the child's point of view in both these novels that adults would miss. Is that why you give them narrative authority?

WC: I'm fascinated with the "liminal state," which I learned about in a graduate class on feminist theory. It's defined as being between two definable states, and childhood is a lot like that. In the first novel, the boy narrator isn't quite in the realm of adulthood, yet. He perceives things but doesn't grasp the full import of them, and that idea of experience and understanding. He's caught somewhere in between.

In my second novel, Easter (who is twelve) knows her dad is a loser, and knows her mom was a drug addict. What I like about coming of age stories is that once you know, you can never "not know." Easter knows these things about her dad, and the novel is about, in some ways, her trying to "unknow" them.

Their powers of rationalization aren't like those of adults. A child can't rationalize violence, cruelty, or addiction. They just know it's there.

AC: The titles of your books have these dark, rhythmic traits.

WC: The first title, *A Land More Kind Than Home,* came from a Thomas Wolfe quote from the closing lines of *You Can't Go Home Again.* I'm a big Thomas Wolfe fan and that quote kind of hints at deliverance, hope for deliverance or a better place beyond the place you are right now. For *This Dark Road to Mercy,* I got the idea in the title from Carson McCullers's *The Ballad of the Sad Café.* There's a quote in that story about two little boys who were orphans and were left to the mercy of the town. So, I thought, this is sort of a travel towards mercy and kind of a road trip novel in a lot of ways. I felt *This Dark Road to Mercy* kind of had a gospel feel to it.

AC: I'm curious about your process of writing your first book.

WC: I started it in 2005 as a short story and I could never get it to work. So, I expanded it and got my first agent by looking at books that I felt were similar to mine. She and I worked on it from 2008 to 2010 roughly. She was never able to sell it so we ended up going separate ways. Around that time, my current agent read an excerpt of the novel in *Crab Orchard Review* and he emailed me and said, "Just give me a call if you ever need an agent." In 2010 I reached out to him and said, "My agent has dropped me. This book is going nowhere. People have rejected it. Will you take a look at it?" and he said, "Yeah." So, he and I kind of went back and forth for a couple of months and then he sold it for a book deal.

AC: And now there's a film option on your second novel?

WC: I'm fortunate that my agent has a close connection and relationship with a film agent in LA. *Million Dollar Baby, LA Confidential*—those were his writers. My literary agent is kind of old school, New York publishing and he doesn't get excited until it is time to get excited. When *The Dark Road to Mercy* came out, that was what they always felt like was the most film-ready. We got serious interest in the option by a German director named Matthias Emcke. And the producer backing it is named David Giler, who wrote and produced *Alien, Predator, Prometheus,* and all these huge science fiction blockbusters and I thought, "What in the world does he want with my book?" But I soon learned that Matthias was the one who really wanted to adapt and direct it. He just needed the financial backing to do it. I've been in touch with Matthias constantly, talking about location and casting. The script is now out for studio backing. I think it's a great script. He made good choices about how to compress a lot of the book into a script. I'm excited, you know, but I'm just cautiously excited.

AC: Cautiously?

WC: That this is going to happen. There's no illusions about any of that. But it would be great. If this had happened five years ago, that would be all I was thinking about. I have been doing this for a little while now, and I have enough friends whose books have been optioned every year for forty years. I just sort of look at it as a tiny bit of income.

AC: I read that you gave up a full-time teaching position to write. How have you looked back on that decision?

WC: I was teaching at a little college in West Virginia. I love my colleagues, and I am still so close to a lot of them and I miss them deeply. It was a small little village; mostly faculty lived there. So, you were just constantly around your friends. There was always somebody around to do something with and I miss that a lot. But people don't realize how much teaching four classes a semester takes out of you. Two of them were composition so I had fifty essays—four to five page essays—to grade and respond to every week. I would have a creative writing class and a literature class with as many as forty students in it. So, I was constantly grading and constantly preparing teaching notes, and then you have the committee work, you have the service to the university, your college, and then you have your own publication schedule you're trying to maintain. Those kinds of things. And I found that my summers were literally eaten up with writing. It's great to have summers off, but it's like a true, double-edged sword when you have summers off and you don't really do anything except write and wait for your wife to come home from work.

AC: And you don't want that to be the only time you can write, because as a writer, you want to do it all year.

WC: Exactly. I just felt really smothered and really pressured. My wife got a job in Morgantown, so my last year at the college I was living about an hour-and-a-half south and that commute made it easier to say, "I can't do this." We had to make that income up somehow. I just put everything I had into it. I resigned before my book came out.

AC: So you didn't resign because of this book; you resigned because of the writing?

WC: Well, my book had sold. But that wasn't enough money to live on indefinitely if I never sold another book. So, I just thought I'd give it a shot, just to see. And maybe, if it doesn't work out I can get another job teaching. My wife said, "Do it. You at least need to take a year and do it." So, my book came out in April 2012, and I was about to leave on this two-month-long book tour. Once I saw the travel that I had gotten myself into I thought, "I came at this at the right time. I can't deal with carrying around papers and stuff." I do miss that ebb and flow of the semester. I do miss the feeling of the first day of summer, the last week of school in May and how everybody is so happy. There are cookouts and parties. I was treated incredibly well and given a lot of space to do what I needed to do. And when I resigned everybody was super supportive and understanding.

AC: Let's talk about your writing routine. It seems like there was very little time between the release of the first novel and the second. Are you a fast writer?

WC: Since the [second] book came out I've been on the road so much and I'm glad that I've had all the time before *A Land More Kind Than Home* was released to write a lot of my second novel. I would have been in trouble otherwise. For me, it seems that there was a long time between them. After the first novel came out I was on the road for half of May, all of June, and half of July. And then the paperback came out in January and I was on the road for half of January, all of February, all of March, and some of April. I had the summer in West Virginia and then we moved to North Carolina around September. We moved into our new house in November. We were living with my wife's parents. So, I didn't have a dedicated writing space, a dedicated time. I had a really hard time getting into a schedule.

I had a local woodworker make me this huge desk out of black walnut that kind of curves around me and I am so in love with it. I have my own office. It is my space and that was the first time that I had that. My normal schedule is: I get up, maybe around 6:30, make coffee, feed the cat, sit on the back deck, read headlines, read sports, read a little bit. My wife leaves for work around eight. I eat breakfast, water the plants, because I've gotten obsessed with gardening now—we have a bigger yard—and then I'm sitting down at the desk about nine and I'll work till noon. I'll try to get a thousand good words that I'm not embarrassed of in those three hours. Then, I'll have lunch, come back, spend the afternoon doing the administrative things. Then I will look back over what I wrote that day and try to find a place to start the next day. I try to be done by the time my wife gets home from work about 5:30. I try to stay away after that. Around the time that the first novel was coming out, I was working...I didn't ever turn it off. If I was at home I was either writing or doing interviews through email, or writing blog posts, writing essays...trying to find ways to get people to buy books. And that is really what I dedicated a whole year to. I'm getting better now at working only when I have to work.

AC: I just finished Amy Greene's *Long Man* and I can't stop thinking about it. What is the last book that you've read that affected you that way?

WC: Gail Godwin's novel *Flora*. I think she is maybe eighty-four-years old and still is at the height of her power. That novel was exceptional. A book by a writer named Smith Henderson called *Fourth of July Creek* is exceptional. I read a lot of stuff for blurbs. I'm kind of overwhelmed with those right now. You know, one of the craziest, most out-of-sight reading experiences I've had in years was *Lonesome Dove* while in Hawaii for a couple of weeks and I loved it.

AC: Writers hate this question but I'll ask it anyway: what are you working on now?

WC: I've kind of been going around and around about it, but it is about a true mill strike that happened back in 1929 that nobody talks about. It's very scandalous. One of the leaders of the strike—maybe the face of the strike—was named Ella May Wiggins, who came down from Sevierville [Tennessee]. She was born in 1900 and found her way to Gastonia and worked in a mill, and from the time she was twenty-eight-years old in 1929 she had nine children. Four of them had died from rickets or the whooping cough or starvation. Her husband had left her and she was living in a predominantly African-American community in a little town called Bessemer City right outside of Gastonia. When this mill strike happened she joined it, because she needed more money, regular working hours, and better conditions at the mill. She ended up trying to integrate the labor union with a communist labor union from New York. She testified in D.C. in front of Congress about the conditions in the South and the plight of working mothers. She wrote these mill ballads that were recorded by Woody Guthrie and Pete Seeger.

She ended up being murdered leaving a protest rally. Some people hired by the mill to turn this caravan of strikers around shot into the caravan. She was shot and killed. She disappeared from history after that.

AC: What writers inspire you? Who just makes you want to write?

WC: I've been inspired by writers on the page and off the page. On the page—Thomas Wolfe, Faulkner to a certain degree. I think it's easy to fall under the sway of Faulkner. Toni Morrison. Most of the writers I've met have just been so overwhelmingly kind to me, especially as a new writer when they didn't have to be. Like Ron Rash, Lee Smith, Gail Godwin, Fred Chappell, Ben Fountain, and Jess Walter. These are people who have gone out of their way to make me feel included. And, it means so much. It makes me feel really welcomed, like I can really do this. I've never felt like, "Oh, here comes the new guy trying to join the club." I've never felt like that. My wife never felt like that.

If you look around, there are many Southern writers who are about my age who are trying to make a go at this. So, I feel like we're all together at a good time. It's a good time to be a new Southern writer between thirty and fifty. ■

BODY OF WATER

LAURA MICHELE DIENER

I need to write a poem about a body of water and I found the task too easy because my body is water.

And because we all try to return home I now live on the water.

And every morning and every evening I walk along the river that divides prosperous states into impoverished ones and I clearly live on the impoverished side because how else could I afford waterfront property?

So I drink in this impoverishment every day, allowing it to ease down the twisting tangles that empty into my womb, where it conducts its little ravages like a jealous nursemaid, and, heedless mother that I am, say nothing.

For there are poisonous loves and poisonous lovers that with one careless joining can become poisonous fathers.

And despite knowing that full well, we bear children into our own loneliness as a balm for or soul-scars, as if we could ever heal scars which have long ago ripped the threads of our construction and we have tried clumsily to darn them into seamlessness but can only approximate the original design.

So every morning and every evening I walk long the banks of the Ohio River, just like in that old song of love and loss and murder, a song that speaks of water but emerged from the people who worked inside the earth.

As I hum this song to myself, perhaps I plan my own little unwitting murders, which is to say, I want a child.

I want to bear a child on this poisoned bank blooming with chemical flowers, this bank, both where I live and my own surface—each sprouting their unnatural gardens of too electric violets, clovers, and buttercups, and other things that blossom in the wild. ■

CANEBREAKS

DEVIN KELLY

Ma first caught me ashing a cigarette off to the side of the old home where the creek rustled through the canebreaks. She said I didn't teach you to treat yourself like that. She said you always got yourself tied to things that'll kill you without knowing. She said death creeps up like a pale horse till you're brokebacked bending over to pick up dandelions for the one you love and then you wind up on your back dead and roasting with your arms across your chest and those same flowers tucked into the breast pocket of your only suit and no one sees fit to carry you they're all too busy saying I told you so.

On the side of the road now few years later ashing a cigarette. The Shenandoah nuzzles into sugar hills and valleys like an old cat sleeping in the dark. Cars come by like little moving stars in the distance then grow until full and blinding and rushing past. Haven't yet made out a face and have since stopped trying. Low mountains all shadow shaped reminding me of Ceels. The way her breasts looked silhouetted under the sheets and the knowing that she was naked underneath, our feet playing small pianos against each other. Kicking the asphalt for losing her. Thinking how the worst last memory to hold of a woman is her taillights spilling all red into the fog telling you to stop giving chase not to even bother. And pops is dying a hundred miles away and there's not a car in sight on my side of the highway. It's black and darker black and different shades of shapes. Nothing to hold me back is what I say.

So I get in my car and figure it is what it is. Think of how some old teach told me time is what you make of it and I figured then as I figure now that it's not doing me no favors. Run my fingers against this patched thing I call a beard and take a pull from a bagged High Life and light another cigarette and can't figure why I stopped in the first place to lean up against the car like it was some broke thing and light up my face red and gold in the night counting stars and always losing the count of things before I even moved my eyes.

Catch sight of my own eyes in the rearview and take a time more than a moment to look into them. People always told me they were mother's. Like she had taken out her own and popped them into my skull when I came wet and crying out of her. Like us boys born with two holes where our eyes supposed to be, figuring mum or pop is just going to pluck out their own and give them away and then pull two of the garden variety out their back pocket. Thinking how my ma had to be one of the two or three most beautiful women in the valley. And remembering the other day when that phone rang how she was running her fingers through her own mother's jewelry box like those necklaces and gemstones were just beaded caterpillars crawling and flipping from finger to finger. The phone between that sharp collarbone and her still taut cheek with her fingers outstretched and her face reflecting off some

And remembering the other day when that phone rang how she was running her fingers through her own mother's jewelry box...

old silver sitting on the mantle I always got to forgetting about polishing as a child, not knowing whose it was and why it was there not serving no purpose. And the way her eyes the ones I got in my head, the way they filmed over like some river was washing over them from the inside. And I not knowing much, not knowing who was saying what. But just how she put that phone down and said your father ain't got much time left and then sitting all quiet with those ruby reds and turquoises and pale white orbs floating around her fingers like they were alive and she wasn't and how she just sat still for an hour or two or more forgetting about the oil popping in the kitchen and watching that hour or two of time age her face in the silver till it looked like she was looking at no one she had ever known.

I remembered after that hour or two or more she said you better go see him.

Don't say I told you, she said.

Just go, she said.

■ ■ ■

when my girl left me i was taking pulls
from the champagne of beers with one foot
up against the frame of the house.

with one foot up against the frame
of the house i was taking pulls from the champagne
of beers when my girl left me.

■ ■ ■

Pops is dying southwest of me just underneath the border of Tennessee in the shadow of Iron Mountain near the Cherokee Forest where Ceels and I once went. We crossed the border to North Carolina and climbed up near Grandfather Mountain and stopped once so she could go barefoot. Walked across that swinging mile high bridge over the gorge. I held her over the edge and can still hear her saying as we both swung like birds on a wire she was saying don't let go don't let go. How there was one moment where some echo of movement caught her voice and all I heard was the let go. Let go, let go. We climbed up the rest of that mountain and sat atop and took deep drags of a few cigarettes and long gulps of wine in flasks. That was her idea. She was like that. Kinda woman you figure might just up and take flight. Sprout wings and go and then fly circles around you smiling like she didn't do nothing wrong. But it was me who lost you, Ceels. That's what I'm thinking to myself now heading south on this road of shadow shapes.

When we were up there looking over Tennessee to our west and Virginia like some angry brother up north, Ceels took to saying things.

I get to thinking what I want, baby, and I can't think of much.

I want to be the rustle in your trees, Ceels.

She grinned, I remember, and took a drag and shook her head like a wet dog.

You always get to thinking about sex, Gilly. That ain't what I want right now. I'm trying to think about what I want.

I took a finger then and thread it through the belt loops of her jeans and plucked a thicket of grassy weed peeking from the rocks behind me and thrust it at her like some waist high boy begging for a peck on the cheek. She slapped me away and that's when I got to knowing she was serious. Her eyes heavy-like, eyelids fluttered like drapes in a breeze.

She said Gilly you gonna be stuck here for all of time. I need to go.

That's what she said. She started chewing on them stalks I plucked for her and I wanted to kiss her full on the lips. Wanted to make her stay a little bit longer. I just shook my head.

She said Gilly I don't know what I want but I'm too beautiful to be made for certain things.

Fog came up high steaming like a slow train from between the trees. I remember thinking that all time did to us was make us sad. I remember wishing I could hold on to one thing forever so that when I took to looking at it or touching it or kissing it full that I could forget about time for awhile. Forget about what sadness was. Sometimes in my dreams there was this bird circling me and laughing with some sort of sharp cackle. Sometimes in my dreams there was that same bird and me pulling out a rifle from under my pillow and laying it to rest and eating it with my bare hands. Ceels was always talking about her dreams. I never placed much stake in them.

■ ■ ■

and the girl i know
    played a cello had to hold it
where my organ supposed to be
    her legs spread and that dirty beast
sad humming into the walls
    you get to thinking what sadness
is what makes a sad sound sad
    and there's the girl i love long gone
legs wide long bowing the things
    we had into music and it gets
to me that i might never know
    what's playing in her mind when
she closes her eyes and if she still
    thinks of how me and her ran away from
a storm soft grey brewing over the hills
    the rain some whisper tickle on our
spines until we collapsed in dirty soil
    and clenched our fists round sweetgrass
as we made love the thunder in the distance
    like angel drums the trees split bowed
and playing the wind like ancient cellos
    her legs spread and our organs pumping
music closing our eyes to keep out the pain
    opening them to keep the nightmares from coming in

■ ■ ■

But I'm here driving to see my dying pops and I get to shaking my head because I should be thinking about him and trying to figure out what kind of memories I should keep for when he might up and leave this earth. I don't have time to waste my time thinking about a girl. That's what I figure. I pull a crooked cigarette from my shirt pocket and light it with both eyes on the road and the smoke curls all up into the nooks of the car. Makes me feel like I'm in a cloud. Still those shadow shapes I'm flying past still those stars appearing around the black bends of roads and then coming at me thinking maybe I might make a wish on the next one I see.

I think about how once Ceels left there was just ma and me. My pops over a hundred miles south keeping to his own. Used to think maybe if I strained my ears I could hear his dog yapping and his rifle sharp shooting into the quiet. But they were other dogs and other guns. Think about what names I do know in this world. Start to list them in my mind as I pass

I pull a crooked cigarette from my shirt pocket and light it with both eyes on the road and the smoke curls all up into the nooks of the car.

mile markers one by one. Ma, Pop, Ceels. Ranger, that's pop's dog. Jesse down at the diner down the road manning the grill and the counter at the same time. Sometimes in the summer he rings up to my house and asks me for a hand and I get to flip eggs and cut through piles of taters with my spatula and take to smelling of butter and grease and coffee. There was that old woman always around the place named Susie who I would've married if I could've been sure she would've made it a few more years. Her and that potato skin all cratered and still beautiful. Hair all bunned up and still glowing almost gold like it forgot she was old. Knew back in her day she turned the whole county's head. Sometimes Ceels would come in and plant a red lipstick kiss on Susie's cheek and it'd leave that perfect lip mark and Susie would wear it around all day like she just got pinned first place in the Miss America contest. My boss at the plow lot, Ephraim. He was alright. Put the whole load of chew in his cheek like he knew any moment might be his last. But he was the one that taught me how to man the plow, twist it round the mountain roads. Taught me how to put whiskey in my hot coffee those winter mornings. Enough to make it burn, that's what he said. I think now about how I loved those roads. Loved plowing the snow and the long line of cars all patient and quiet not even honking knowing I was just doing my job. Knowing I was depended on. Knowing even when Ceels left, burning faint glowing red into the quiet fog, that I had to get up the next morning because at least someone needed me. But hell that hurt. Ephraim said there was nothing a little more whiskey couldn't fix but Ephraim was wrong. Spitting out black spit choking on his big cancer throat. Think now about if Ephraim ever knew what love was and how it could still make me hard in the dark orange of a morning twisting around a mountain road at twenty an hour pushing away a foot of snow in a rust truck between big gulps with all these husbands and wives and sons and daughters in a curving mechanical line behind me like where they had to go meant something and I was just a nuisance they had to bear.

Fifty miles to go and the morning sun is bleeding into the sky like skin cut underwater. Floating oranges and yellows and reds and purples seeping into the fog over mountain shapes. Canebrakes patching up the side of the long road like cat fur on a dark shirt.

■ ■ ■

mother this is me talking can you hear
you are from the land of fast moving women
but you are the only one still here

making coffee in the mornings
and singing something to a spirit ghost
who stands beside you

all the other boys needed their hands on metal
but i had my hands in dirt mother are you
supposed to tell me who it is i am supposed

to love or what or when before the world
leaves me in one direction or another
pulling my pants up from around my ankles

■ ■ ■

Pull into a gas station where the gas used to be ninety-nine cents a gallon and my pops would let me pump it while he stepped inside and bought me a sleeve of Necco Wafers which I popped one by one into my mouth until my tongue was chalk and my voice was sweet. Station is right next to an adult store that juts out of a strip club where I walk in because even though it's early morning it's still open and I'm hungry for something good and I just want to sit quick and have a bite and look up at these women and take my mind off Ceels. Pops joked he used to take me to strip joints when I was too small to remember and a few times when I did remember and he'd sit me up on his knee and the women would come almost kiss his cheek and then talk to me like mothers and stroke my hair and he said I helped lower the price of a few too many lap dances. He was a few beers deep when he said that but I took it to be a little more than true.

But now I'm sitting off from the stage with a bloody burger and a cigarette smoking from an ashtray. Just one woman on the stage. I see her through the smoke and she looks like she could be a dream, all sticky-like and not really there and moving like a cloud of fog just all hips and legs. There can't be more than four people in the whole place. I wonder if I got a bit of food stuck in my half-beard. I sit back and watch this girl move without looking at her face. All a sudden those legs soft-swaying to my table and her whisper in my ear.

What's your name, she says.

I say Gilly.

I ask what's yours.

Daisy, she says.

Like the flower?

Yes. It's just barely a whisper, her voice is.

Is that your god-given name, I say.

She says I don't believe in no god.

I say what do you believe in. What is your name from birth.

She says I don't remember.

Well, what do you remember?

She says I remember you told me you got something to forget.

I ain't never been around here.

I seen you.

But I ain't.

I look up and her eyes are big wide things like double moons paned through the glass. Kinda eyes make you fall in love and then drown and die. Eyes like Ceels'. Dark and wide. Eyes like river water at night. She got on these baby blue high laced boots and she's all glittered up and shining bending over me like starlight on creek beds. She leans into my ear.

You got a favorite song, she says.

I think for a minute. All my favorite songs these finger-picked things. I think of an old folk one. Something bout a miner singing how his love would drive him to blast through mountains for his woman. Something bout how his woman got trapped, then, in a mountain, how he was just talking shit.

I tell Daisy this and she puts it on and then she is up on that stage dancing slow and smooth like honey dripping from a spoon and something like smoke gets all up in the room and I think about crying. I think how if my pops was here how he might slip a crinkled five into my palm and grin. Think of how the only time I remember seeing my pops get a lap dance, how I asked how come I didn't see mom do that to him and how he grinned again and said just cause you don't see it don't mean it don't happen.

Daisy still dancing now and I reach into my wallet for some crusty bill and all I got is a ten so I leave it on the foot of the stage and when I turn from the door as I leave she is still dancing and looking at the place I just left. I figure we are all dancing for people who aren't there no more. I stop for a second before I get in the car and smoke a cigarette and try to get sad. I don't. Ceels is so far gone. She's in New York somewhere. All I've got is a receipt for a pack of beer and two frosted doughnuts with her number on the back scrawled and somehow fading. It smells like the weed I tried to roll up in it before I realized I still loved her and always will.

■ ■ ■

low whistle moan and i pull up my jeans
i do not know if one precedes the other
i do not know much of anything

in another life a teacher once told me
i could have been a gunslinger
but i said a gunslinger has always got to move

and i got nowhere i want to go

■ ■ ■

Crossing the border into Tennessee now. Morning sun sitting half mooned atop the mountains. Everything reminds me of someone and I wonder if this is how it is for everyone. Mother is just now waking up putting coffee in the filter for the ten thousandth time. The little fabric strands from her nightgown dragging along the floor with her bare feet. She is a strong woman I can say that and feel the truth pouring out of me. I do not think she ever gave that man my pops a lap dance. She is holding her mug with two hands looking out the window over the sink. I never knew what she was thinking then.

What's it gonna be, Gilly? She said one morning.

Eggs, ma.

Gilly. What's it gonna be?

Just eggs, ma.

Oh, Gilly. Gilly.

Everything reminds me of someone and I wonder if this is how it is for everyone.

That morning there was a deer dead in the snow I was plowing along the bare tree roads. I am strong and I could have stepped out of the cab of the truck to move it with some kind of dignity to the side of the road. But I just kept plowing. It made a thud when its cold bones pushed up against my plow. I pushed it along for a few miles before it fell off to the side around a bend. I knew then that I would never leave this place. I broke two of my fingers pounding them into the wheel when my shift was over. That night I pushed those two fingers up inside Ceels and she asked why I was wincing. I said because it hurts to please you, Ceels. And she grabbed me by my hips and said rut me Gilly, rut me until you die from all the pain.

Pop's house stands like it always did. Like it might blow over when a train comes past. But sometimes the strongest dogs are standing on three legs. There is my knock on the door and my waiting and the silence of no answer moving all the way through me. I light a cigarette but it canoes and I crunch it with my boot instead of making it right.

Ma must be sitting at the kitchen table on her second mug. I wonder if she ever lifts her nightgown over her thin hair and touches herself and thinks of someone else. Someone she might have never got a chance with. Something in me hopes she does because something in me knows she deserves at least that. She was born to watch people leave. All mothers are, I think.

Pops is dead when I jiggle the doorknob and let myself in with a hard push from a bent shoulder. He is leaned up against a few pillows in his bed surrounded by unfinished things. I go up and touch him on his shoulder.

Pops, I say.

There is a scratching sound coming from the other room. Something almost jarring. I walk in and there is the needle of his record player scratching circles around the groove where no song plays. Just circling something mad. For who knows how long, I wonder. I put the needle back in its right place and there is a folk song something soft-picked coming through his ratty speaker cages. I think of pops alive years ago strumming faint on the porch as the wind came and rustled through the canebrakes like brush drums. I think of him singing to me something tender and then going inside to beat on my mother. I figure all people got at least two sides to them.

I sit by his side for some time and drink from his half done cup of cool coffee. I put some whiskey in it and talk to my father.

What killed you, pops, I say.

Was it me?

Sometimes I think he answers but when I look I see he is still not breathing. He looks alright in death, I think. I push his eyelids down and his skin is like canvas stretched across his drawn face. The slow slope of his gut still visible under the blanket. I take some clippers and groom his toenails like he would do late at night while I was fast asleep. Then I start to cry. A low whistle hums through the wood of the walls. I think of everyone passing here and not knowing. I think of ma on her fourth cup and Ceels walking some city street and how it is just me and my father in a slatted house down in Tennessee. The train comes crying past sounding different when it comes than when it goes and I know it is not crying for me or pops. I button my father's shirt to its top button and cross his hands across his chest and go outside to pick a flower for him to carry with him into the beyond. But there are only canebrakes in his dirt yard. Those flowers that even in life look more dead than alive. I bushel a few together. They smell like coal dust and cigarettes. I wrap his fingers round their thin stems and the top of one tickles his nose and I wonder if he can feel that tickle wherever he might be now.

Ceels, I say into my end of my father's phone. I am leaned up against the kitchen counter. I can see my father's pale toes pointing up all crooked out from one end of the blanket. I am holding that crunched up wrinkled receipt in the palm of my hand.

Hi Gilly, she says.

Ceels, I say.

Yes, Gilly.

My pops is dead.

Oh, Gilly.

Don't you want to say you're sorry?

Gilly I got something to tell you.

Can't you just say you're sorry for me?
Gilly, I'm carrying a child.
What was that?
Gilly, I'm pregnant.
Is it mine? Is it my child?
Yes, Gilly.
Is it a boy? Is it my boy?
I don't know yet, Gilly.
When will you know if it's my boy?
I don't know, Gilly.
Are you gonna keep it?
I don't think so, Gilly. I don't think so.

■ ■ ■

Daisy is still there in the full sun of the morning streaming high beamed through the misty fog of the foothills. She is still there on that stage dancing. The room still empty, me still ashing a cigarette. Thinking of how it was like I never left. Those three men still sitting in those three same chairs all around the place. One of those places where time doesn't exist. But Daisy is moving and I walk up to her and sit down at the foot of the stage. I ask her to play that same song from earlier. It is slow and scratchy and she is covered in an inch of shining sweat. She moves like a storm cloud around the top of a mountain. Soon, I think, I will be swallowed whole. I took all of my father's money when I left him there, eyes closed, holding canebrakes, feeling tickled in some other life. He would have wanted me to. I take a few crumpled twenties and motion for Daisy. I slip them into the strap of her thong. She smiles. She bends over and kisses me on the cheek and runs one hand from my ear to my chin. This is what it feels like, I think, to know you will be in one place for the rest of time. ■

TO GET INSIDE SOMETHING

If people all over the country sat praying for bus stops
it would look like people waiting for the bus.

I have to let my boundary down,
to feel these people inside their glass case
and not hover outside the prayer container.

I don't know how to pray.
I am a slug, unexposed.

An enormous black man stands at the bus stop
in a football jersey.
The man has a bleached stripe on his neck,
a quick drawing born on his skin
or a space for someone trying to get out.
I try to pray for the drawn skin-door and keep shifting
to the parked cars behind it.
Scar car draw prayer scare. Bus brakes come.

I don't want to crack open,
crash, peel inside-out into sky.

COURTNEY MANDRYK

OUR BONES LIKE STARS LIKE MILK

I can feel when the baby enters sleep
his consciousness departing
as his brain unzips.

Sometimes I follow him there, as if he has sucked me in.
We know nothing. I am a speck of a speck of a star
here in this insignificant house.

At the bus stop is a shopping cart, but no stores
for at least a mile, carts
dropped off here like a stepchild from another planet
mother
God bus Rosie stop.

A girl approaches as we pass. She is younger than I am by
a decade,
too thin and half-black with a short ponytail.
Three of her would fit Rosie.
Her legs don't work right, one knee-bone leaning into the
other.

Do any of you got a cigarette I can buy?

Husband says no, and she looks neither disappointed nor
surprised.
Aww, she says loudly to the baby, loud enough that he stirs
in his sleep.

I don't know
how to pray for the beauty of a stranger, bones unknown,
but simile is prayer. Like Rosie. Like Rosie I pray for her,
the prayer emerging from a place inside that feels like a
    bone that is broken.

COURTNEY MANDRYK

BREACH

Once, I came to your room
to roll the sheets down

to your collarbone groove
above the moon-shaped scar

your mother left. In the cool
gnaw of hard wood, I bent

to both knees, cradled your hand
like a dead mouse, stroked from head

to tail. Under canvas-stretched lids,
your eyes wandered

and this: I thought I saw
on the belly of your blink,

feathers floating tied to a string
I prayed to your god I could pull.

CHRISTEN NOEL

THE LAST TIME I SAW ANNA SANCHEZ

When they splayed her out like a fish
no one said a word.
We were raised for silence.

Two trucks rolled by on Interstate 71
to some northern place.
I wanted to move with them
to Lake Erie or across the Canadian border.
We were all fighting border wars.
I should have told her before that night
how the boys would smile
when they heard her roll her r's.

Sometimes I go to the river
to cut the fisherman's nets.
I make girl-shaped holes in the woven rope,
pretend it is enough
as slick bodies fight to break free,
reflecting the moon on their scales.

CHRISTEN NOEL

TRAGEDY
ON A LARGE STAGE

GENEVIEVE THURTLE

In Raymond Carver's iconic "What We Talk About When We Talk About Love," the two couples at the center of the narrative never leave the kitchen table, and yet, over the course of its fifteen pages, the story dangles these characters over a dark existential abyss. Alice Munro's "Runaway" places its protagonist, a young woman trapped in a bad and potentially voilent marriage, on a small, claustrophobia-inducing ranch. Amy Hempel's "The Cemetery Where Al Jolson is Buried" takes place almost entirely in a character's hospital room, where the protagonist fails to provide her best friend, who is dying of cancer, the abiding love and devotion she yearns for in her final days. Contemporary short fiction often grapples with the intimate tragedies that occur within the four walls of a bedroom, a hospital waiting room, or a kitchen. These stories illustrate the quiet sensibility of modern short fiction: one of intimacy, of those barely visible tremors that hint at the seismic subterranean shifts of human love and allegiance, of treachery and howling grief.

The central tragedy in Tim O'Brien's "How to Tell a True War Story," however, plays out on a larger stage—the maddening, chaotic, blood-soaked theater of Vietnam. And yet, O'Brien's work is no less intimate than Carver's or Munro's or Hempel's. In this eighteen-page work, O'Brien attempts to capture the slippery nature of war stories by telling, and re-telling, the story of Curt Lemon, a young field grunt who loses his life to a landmine. O'Brien uses this anchoring narrative as a way to define the outer edges of the "true" war story, in all of its contradictions, ironies, and embellishments of memory. Returning to Curt Lemon's death as the story's touchstone, O'Brien deals with the tragedy and nihilism of war by slowly revealing, in intimate detail, its true, horrifying face.

The reader first learns of Curt Lemon's death from Tim O'Brien, the story's fictional narrator, a man twenty years removed from his stint in Vietnam. During a respite between travel and battle, O'Brien's unit catches some R and R under a serene jungle canopy. While the ill-fated Curt Lemon and his friend, Rat Kiley, toss around a harmless smoke grenade, O'Brien remembers a "soft dripping sound somewhere beyond the trees...that trail junction and those giant trees...[and] the smell of moss. Up in the canopy there were tiny white blossoms, but no sunlight at all...Except for the laughter things were quiet."[1] In this prelude to Lemon's death, O'Brien merges the lyrical and the ominous. While he remembers the "smell of moss" and the "tiny white blossoms," he also recalls the sweetly sickening "soft dripping sound" in the trees that foreshadows the gore of Lemon's death, the blood and guts of his decimated body. Even the silence that is punctuated by Kiley and Lemon's laughter is menacing and ironic in this volatile, unpredictable landscape. This moment is the proverbial calm-before-the-storm in a world where human joy and pleasure have no place.

With this setting established, O'Brien proceeds to narrate the first version of Lemon's death. He remembers:

> *[they] were just goofing around. There was a noise, I suppose, which must've been the detonator, so I glanced behind me and watched Lemon step from the shade into bright sunlight. His face was suddenly brown and shining. A handsome kid, really. Sharp gray eyes, lean and narrow-waisted, and when he died it was almost beautiful, the way the sunlight came around him and lifted him up and sucked him high into a tree full of moss and vines and white blossoms.*[2]

This unlikely version of Lemon's death is oddly pastoral, "almost beautiful," a reflection of the setting O'Brien establishes just a paragraph earlier. In this passage, Lemon's death is biblical in nature; he is "shining" like the mythical, ascended Christ who is brought up to the heavens enveloped in light. And just like the risen Christ, Curt Lemon, in this first version of his death, is whole, intact, still handsome, still in possession of his youthful beauty. He resides in the tree with its moss, vines and white blossoms. In this version, there is no mention of death itself. Instead, O'Brien renders him a fairy-tale figure who defies the laws of physics and mortality. And yet, the reader thinks, this cannot be what really happened. This cannot be a "true" war story.

O'Brien addresses this concern in the subsequent paragraph, a meditation on the nature of war stories. "In any war story," O'Brien writes, "but especially a true one, it's difficult to separate what happened from what seemed to happen. What seems to happen becomes its own happening and has to be told that way."[3] The slippery nature of narrative truth becomes even more so when memory comes into play, according to O'Brien. What is remembered, whether accurate or not, becomes one form of truth, memory's truth. And what is remembered about a traumatic, horrific event, like the violent death of a friend, can be quite different than how it objectively happened. O'Brien seems to suggest that the mind has its own form of self-protection. It can embellish a memory with details that soften, or make beautiful, an event that is the polar opposite of beautiful. It can transform death and dismemberment into resurrection. This is memory's truth—a truth far more potent than objective truth, in O'Brien's estimation.

The "truth" of Curt Lemon's death evolves, however, in its second telling eight pages later. O'Brien acknowledges that he has "told [the story] before—many times, many versions—but here's what actually happened."[4] O'Brien identifies, in

1 Tim O'Brien. *The Things They Carried* (New York: Broadway Books, 1990), 70.
2 Ibid.
3 Ibid., 71.
4 Ibid., 78.

one of the story's many metafictive gestures, the distinction between "memory truth" and "real truth," setting up the reader's expectation of a story that lays bare the true horror of Lemon's demise, a horror strikingly absent from the story's first iteration. This new, "truer" version, however, has its own sense of unreality: "We crossed the river and marched west into the mountains. On the third day, Curt Lemon stepped on a booby-trapped 105 round. He was playing catch with Rat Kiley, laughing, and then he was dead. The trees were thick; it took nearly an hour to cut an LZ for the dustoff."[5] Completely absent from this second version are the lyrical language and long, complex sentences of the first. Instead, this version possesses a clipped, clinical tone. The passage is devoid of the evocative, emotional layer of the first version. O'Brien doesn't appear to narrate from the first-person perspective as he does earlier, a move that creates distance between the narrator and Lemon's death. In fact, the narrative distance here is so great that the reader has little sense of the details surrounding the accident. The reader knows that Lemon unwittingly detonates a mine—O'Brien even specifies the type—and he also knows Lemon dies—both details missing from the first telling. But these added details do little to inform us of "what actually happened." Although stripped of the fanciful and "unrealistic" details of the first version, this version possesses so few details, realistic or not, that it seems like a mere sketch of the event. As a result, it strikes the reader as just as "untrue" in its own way as the first version, yet another construct of a self-protective psyche that cannot confront the truth of Lemon's end, in all of its unfathomable devastation. What also strikes the reader is this version's emptiness and pointlessness. In the first version, the aesthetic beauty of the passage redeems the subject matter—Lemon's death—in the post-modernist sense that language possesses a redemptive power that nothing else does in our modern age of disillusionment. Its beauty alone makes it worthy. In the second version, however, Lemon's death is met with no redemption; O'Brien attaches no meaning to it whatsoever, and the reader is left to confront the emptiness of this world O'Brien's soldiers inhabit.

In subsequent paragraphs, O'Brien goes on to discuss more characteristics of the true war story, one of which is meaninglessness. In a true war story, he says, "there is not even a point...The war's over. You close your eyes. You smile and think, Christ, what's the point?"[6] O'Brien recognizes the emptiness in death, particularly death wrought by war, and he maintains this nihilistic view in the story's third, more graphic version of Lemon's death:

> *In the mountains that day, I watched Lemon turn sideways. He laughed and said something to Rat Kiley. Then he took a peculiar half step, moving from shade into bright sunlight, and the booby-trapped 105 round blew him into a tree. The parts were just hanging there, so Dave Jensen and I were ordered to shinny up and peel him off. I remember the white bone of an arm. I remember pieces of skin and something wet and yellow that must've been intestines. The gore was horrible, and stays with me. But what wakes me up twenty years later is Dave Jensen singing "Lemon Tree" as we threw down the parts.*[7]

Here, O'Brien returns to the more overt subjectivity of the first-person perspective. The narrative distance that

5 Ibid.
6 Ibid., 82.
7 Ibid., 82-83.

dominated in the second version is replaced by O'Brien's undeniable inhabiting of this reality. In fact, half of this telling focuses on the narrator as he recovers Lemon's remains—an event that was absent from the earlier iterations of the story. This telling includes O'Brien's reaction to Lemon's death, how the gore stayed with him, and the long-lasting impact of Dave Jensen's joking rendition of a song that has Lemon's last name, the moment that, he claims, still "wakes me up." O'Brien reveals Lemon's death in all of its ghastliness, sparing no gory detail. Lemon's is a body ruined, annihilated senselessly, not in battle, but by his unfortunate, inauspicious footing. There is no meaning to be found here, O'Brien ultimately concludes—no glory, no heroism, no redemptive lesson. And what follows Lemon's annihilation is the harming of yet more people, the soldier O'Brien and his partner Jensen, two young men who have the great misfortune of being chosen to deal with the gruesome aftermath of this moment. O'Brien the writer makes it clear why the two earlier versions of Lemon's death exist: they reveal the strategies people use to manage their terror and horror. We misremember; we embellish; we generate a psychic chasm between ourselves and the inconceivable, and the senseless. We are just creatures who must survive above all else, O'Brien seems to suggest, even if survival requires evasion and denial.

But O'Brien does not end his story here; he is not yet done telling the tale of Curt Lemon's death. In the story's final iteration, O'Brien admits to not "[getting] the story right," despite his many attempts.[8] O'Brien returns, once again, to the story's touchstone:

> *I can still see the sunlight on Lemon's face. I can see him turning, looking back at Rat Kiley, then he laughed and took that curious half step from*

shade into sunlight, his face suddenly bright and shining, and when his foot touched down, in that instant, he must've thought it was the sunlight that was killing him. It was not the sunlight. It was a rigged 105 round...[The] sun seemed to gather around him and pick him up and lift him high into a tree, if I could somehow re-create the fatal whiteness of the light, the quick glare, the obvious cause and effect, then you would believe the last thing Curt Lemon believed, which for him must've been the final truth.[9]

In this final version, O'Brien merges elements of the previous three. He returns to the sunlight and Lemon's "shining" face of the first version, and he retains the specificity of the mine type and the fatality of Lemon's misstep of the second and third versions. What he leaves out of this final version, of course, is the overwhelming, but entirely realistic, gore of the third iteration. What is new here, however, is O'Brien's attempt to imagine Lemon's internal experience of the fatal explosion, but his inability "to get the story right" prevents him, and the reader, from fully apprehending Lemon's internal state. Ultimately, O'Brien acknowledges the limitations of memory and narrative to capture the "truth" of any story.

As readers, we will never know what Curt Lemon's "final truth" was in the light's "fatal whiteness," only that he was alive and intact one moment and fatally broken the next. The rest of what is known, according to O'Brien, resides in that liminal space between fact and imagination, between confronting the truth and fleeing from it. ■

8 Ibid., 84.
9 Ibid.

EGGSHELLS AROUND THIS HOUSE

unlike fonts forgotten or scripted with shellac   our history

  went along making itself in stray gaps   of what conversation bubbled up

kin to curses uttered ages back   now blue-collar provisions or buried shames unknown

sins committed long before we came   & it wasn't so much the mess but the smell

garbage undiminished   gluts of jerky scraps & ceiling chain hooks   bottle spilt peroxide

& battery acid flaking crust   sharp stink of diluted vodka tonics soaked milky

  on newsprint   silence common as quivers of unfinished arrows

or bowstrings' slacked appetites   or the dank garage hung with stags   & sawed horns or obtuse smiles of load-ready shotguns open   thus we never talked about killing

or the time coming where he knew he would

DAVE HARRITY

MOTHER'S CROSSWORD, #26 DOWN

Like her fingernails, the pencil gnawed & short—
                a tic, her small specter of control. & this thing like letting go:
What's a four letter word for 'assertion or demonstration of power'?
                So few ways to see it otherwise,
with dishes piled up & faucet leaking—her armchair
                session's weekend meditation. After piano, she'd rehash
our own domestic politic, shake her bauble sitting there.
                Which is it? she says to me, *is it 'WARS' or 'GODS,' or 'DADS'?*
Since she was never great with riddles, clandestine interludes—
                never played a mind game in her life. *'VETO'* was the word
I volunteered but she wasn't really all that wrong I guess.

DAVE HARRITY

BLUE DINOSAUR

CHERYL SMART

1. Rob a Townie

I remember stealing only once. It was not the sort of thing a God-fearing girl would normally do. Stealing would set my seven-year-old soul in danger of the Hell fire promised to me every week by Sunday School teachers and weeping pastors pacing the pulpit, raising their Bibles and shaking their heads at the shame of it all. I coveted something deeply though which I knew was a violation of the Ten Commandments and would surely be my doom, but since I had coveted already, why not go ahead and take what I wanted? I had already broken one of the Commandments with just my want. There was never any mention that Hell would be hotter the more Commandments I violated. Only one would suffice.

2. A How-To Guide

I robbed a townie. I argued to God that it was fair anyway because townies had everything. Farm kids had nothing but dirt. Sometimes food grew out of it and we ate. Sometimes it didn't and we got a little hungry now and again. Hunger for nourishment is easier to stifle than the hunger for another life. Never satisfied was my desire to have what other children had. I wanted new jackets and shoes instead of those that were handed down God knows how many times. I wanted clothing that was not handmade by my mother, even though I knew what she created with love and skill, cutting and sewing fabric late into the night, was far superior to anything the townies could order from the Sears & Roebuck catalog. I wanted candy. I wanted toys. I wanted a red skateboard in spite of the reality that there was only dirt and grass and a small concrete porch to scoot it across. I wanted what belonged to my second grade classmate, a dark-haired boy with fair skin and laughing eyes.

On this rainy spring day when I was to become a thief, recess was held indoors. Some of us played Duck-Duck-Goose or I-Spy, some read books, and a few of us gathered around the dark-haired boy as he retrieved a bag of plastic dinosaurs from his backpack. He let the dinosaurs fall onto the mottled grey and blue commercial carpeting that covered a portion of our classroom, and we all began playing with them. They were unnaturally colored things, bright red and green, yellow and blue. We made dinosaur sounds and dying noises when the

Tyrannosaurus Rex killed the smaller dinosaurs. The owner of the dinosaurs made it clear that he was in charge of the T-Rex.

"They're my dinosaurs," he said, "This one is my favorite, but I will share the others."

That was all right with me because I felt a special connection with a blue Stegosaurus that had been cast to the side. I was the only girl in the dinosaur group. The boys shunned my dinosaur noise and play. Even the boy in charge would not use the T-Rex to eat my Stegosaurus although he ate all the other dinosaurs. The boys forgot all about me and the blue Stegosaurus so he and I drifted off into our own dinosaur land, eating grass and chasing imaginary Pterodactyls. All too soon our teacher, Mrs. Clifft, called for clean-up as recess would be over in five minutes. This set us all in gear to be back in our seats on time as Mrs. Clifft was a tyrant, as terrifying as any of those dinosaurs on the floor should they have taken up life in their true forms and began tromping around our classroom crushing victims. Mrs. Clifft crushed victims all the time. With her words. And with a long, thick wooden paddle that lifted me off the floor from the force of it every time she swung it. My petite body suspended itself on tiptoes, and then rocked back onto my heels, only to be raised up again in the next moment by another whack. Sometimes, Mrs. Clifft grabbed my arm and held me in place for paddlings because I was too small to ground and brace myself. I tiptoed, rocked back, stumbled forward. I was all over the place. She learned she could hit me better if she helped me be still for it.

The boys in our group dropped the dinosaurs where they were and left the owner of them to scoop them up on his own. As he deposited them into the clear plastic bag from whence they had come, there was a brief moment the good in me tried to drop the dinosaur into the pile with the others. But my hunger to have it proved too great. I palmed the dinosaur into my hand, walked away, and with all the stealth a fledgling bandit can have, deposited the thing into the slide-out cubby of my desk. I glanced back at my classmate just as he was shoving the other dinosaurs into his backpack, fully expecting that he had noticed the missing stegosaurus and was about to name me a thief to our teacher. That didn't happen. It was easy enough for me to slip my prize into my book satchel at the end of the day. I kept my hand inside my satchel the entire hour-long bus ride home, gripping the toy dinosaur just to be sure of it, not daring to bring it out into the open for any of the other poor kids to claim as I had done. I wrapped my hand tightly around the blue dinosaur, feeling the ridges along its back and the spikes on its tail. I marveled that it was mine.

I kept my hand inside my satchel the entire hour-long bus ride home, gripping the toy dinosaur just to be sure of it...

3. The Drawbacks

When the bus dropped my sister and me at our stop, I ambled along behind her on our walk home, leaving enough space between us so I could enjoy my treasure privately. The sun peaked out from behind a cloud and sparked the auburn highlights of her long, wavy hair. I longed for her dark tresses instead of my own limp, stringy dishwater-colored strands. Come summer, I would at least enjoy the blonde streaks that allowed me to pretend I was a California girl. I envied my sister's beauty. But in that moment, my walk was a little prouder than hers, a little richer, because I had a new friend.

We trekked a half-mile down, down, down the curvy gravel drive that became worse for the wear the closer it snaked toward our farmhouse. The portion of the road owned by the county was well-maintained, with healthy amounts of gravel and properly graded. The road became our actual driveway at the end of it however and those parts were much less rocky, more narrow, and more to the liking of a proper farm girl. I liked the sound and crunch of gravel under my feet.

I walked the gravel road with the blue dinosaur in my hand, as happy as I ever remember being as a child. He and I played dinosaur games all afternoon outside until the sun went down. I imagine feeding the dinosaur bits of turnip greens underneath the table at suppertime, and that being the last bit of our fun together. When dusk settled in, I began to feel the weight of the blue dinosaur. I can feel the weight of it now nearly forty years later.

By bedtime, I felt as heavy as any sinner could feel. I had kept the blue dinosaur with me the whole evening, tucking it into my pants pocket or hiding it inside my small fist whenever my sister or mother came near. No one knew I was a thief. My sister was only a few feet from me in the room we shared as I lay on my back in bed, twirling the dinosaur around and around between my thieving fingers. I was sad the toy had lost its magic. I didn't want to hold the dinosaur anymore or even to look at it. I tucked the thing underneath my mattress and felt the burden of it much like Hans Christian Anderson's princess felt the queen's pea. But never a princess was I. It wasn't the weight of the object that burdened me, but the weight of my sin in taking it. I wanted the blue dinosaur gone. I wanted to hide my sin and shame and never look at it again. I felt the eyes of God on me like I would imagine Adam and Eve must have felt when they had sinned and in realizing it, covered their nakedness before the Almighty. I wanted to cover myself, too. And I wanted to cover the dinosaur and the sin of it forever. I decided to make a holy sacrifice to God of the thing I had coveted and stolen.

4. A Righteous Sacrifice

The next day was a Saturday and at first light, I went outside to make an offering of repentance to the Lord. I told God I was sorry and knowing that He could see straight into my heart, I knew He could see it was true. I buried the tiny, blue dinosaur under the wild cherry tree at the Northwest corner of our farmhouse. My disgrace moved me to hide the thing there in the dirt, as did my desire to never again be tempted by the sight of it. Yet greater than those motivators was the longing for a righteous sacrifice. Even as a child, I knew once a holy sacrifice was offered to God, the thing sacrificed should never be touched by human hands again because to do so would taint the offering.

As far as I know, my sacrifice is still there in the ground underneath the wild cherry tree, along with the piece of myself I offered up to the Lord that spring morning, the piece that begged forgiveness and promised to be an honest girl from then on. The piece that said I wish I hadn't taken the blue dinosaur and broken God's loving commandments. Say what you will about the Lord. But whatever I put into the ground that day, and whatever my heart lifted up to the heavens must have been a powerful thing. The blue dinosaur. It's the only sin I've ever buried. I'm a prolific sinner. I've sinned wide open all my days. It's not the honest transgressions that swallow you up. It's the hidden ones, the dishonest ones. Those are the kind of sins that rattle the devil. ■

COUGAR, BLUE RIDGE

The summer sun is far too high; the wind
is too far down. Alone, I pad a trail
as ancient as these rocks. The caged dogs wail,
are going wild—but I will not be skinned.
Declared extinct this spring. I may be soon—
my leap is less, my stomach almost gone.
I pad alone, lost in the East, icon
of the West. I scream in light of moon
on mountain balds, from caves: my forty names.
I stalk, I crouch, I ambush from behind.
My range is wide. I live alone; don't mind.
I break the neck to kill, ask for no names.
I pad into the dark, no food, no rest.
The end of trail is heavy in my chest.

MAREN O. MITCHELL

CADIZ

There's nothing in this warm, vegetal dusk
That is not beautiful or that will last.
—*Joe Bolton, "Tropical Courtyard"*

At the end of Main Street, the sun pulls the road
downward
a little lower each day, before disappearing in green.
Six storefronts on each side become downward heading
stair steps, a rage against geometry

and the road falls faster than the storefront sidewalk
where old timers pass judgment on the drive through
traffic,
whittle, spit, speak in staccato sentences. Maybe
they've earned their position, having outlasted the rest,
to stay under a wooden awning while the temperature
rises.

Molecules hang in the air and the light disperses.
It is that time washed in a dirty gold patina, when walking
becomes akin to drowning.
Descent pulls
the red needle of an old Fury speedometer further right.
I take my foot off the brake pedal I've been riding
since the city limit sign, looking for some residue
or finger print that is yours. A whitewashed steeple
marks the end of civilization, and across the street
a Texaco station whose metal sign hangs by its last
unbroken finger.

Here, a momentary lapse into acclivity
triggers the thought enough speed could lift a man out
of this town, flying, leave little care for what waited
beneath the camouflage of green maple leaves,
or little care for what waits when the fact of flying ends.

D.A. GRAY

THREE BATTLES IN THE HILL COUNTRY

I.
Back of a rented house its mock-barn roof
warps; paint peels from the eave.

Feeders suspend from what branches remain,
while the severed limbs claim squatter's rights
by the gravel drive. Residue of an evening

thunderstorm gathers in a dead fountain;
bees reclaim the basin's edge
where water pools amid cracks and above,
a plaster Neptune fondles a fish.

The white pine lattice hangs
on a climbing rose, still standing but fallen
so far behind on the rent she no longer cares.

Survivors of the rain season find ways to sleep.

II.
Rains in the hill country create transient
lakes. A neglected Folgers can defines
water into a cylinder; months of frustration

bleed a ferrous beck through its seam.

Fireflies light on the skin of water maple leaves,
unafraid for the first time in years—of Mason jars.

Toad hangs from the storm door, a presence
so silent until,
                    in a flash,
his x-ray outline burns into the dark.

Then,
        thunderclap!

In the quieting aftermath, cricket
strokes her thigh without rosin
moving bullfrog to stutter.

The improvisation of the wild drowns
an Interstate's protracted groan, one mile away.

III.
Television's blue flashes expose ivy skeletons
covering window pains, and beneath the sill

headless prickly pear rises.

A lone pickup truck sits empty on half-flat tires
where honeysuckle sags over the fencerow
like a warning.
                    The owner of the house no longer
ventures past the door, casualty of a lost war.

D.A. GRAY

BOOK REVIEW

William Kelley Woolfitt. *Beauty Strip*. Huntsville, Tex.: Texas Review Press, 2014. 82 pages. Softcover. $19.95.

Reviewed by Sylvia Woods

William Kelley Woolfitt's poetry collection *Beauty Strip* offers a poet's sure touch in language and sound. This full-length poetry collection both celebrates the beauty and history of West Virginia and laments the destruction wrought by outsiders intent on gutting the state's natural resources. Apt biblical and historical references document the struggles and joys of the mountain people, their enduring strength and dignity. By the end of the collection, in the poem "Absentee," there is no doubt that West Virginia has been sacrificed, which "makes an overseas company rich."

The book begins and ends with descriptions of a boy being forced into life in the mines, with images of his hands in "Meditation on a Boy Miner," exploring the boy's dread of the darkness inherent in mine work. Hands ruined, the boy, "clenches his hands,.....the space inside them dark as cave streams, sump/pools, where the spirit broods/before it calls out the light." More optimistic, the final poem describes a thirteen-year-old boy with a kite, who dreams of a girl with freckles with whom to spend his life, "If he goes on running, it will take him to a joy that breaks him."

"Mountain Top Removal Site," explains the meaning behind the title of the book: "We can't see behind the false-fronted hills, beauty strip/they left to hide from us the marks of their labor." The unnamed "they" hide from the residents the destruction they must search to see. Woolfitt interrupts his normal lyrical language with the blunt reminder mountaintop removal mining is based on "cheaper quicker access" in which "450 mountains" and "2400 miles of streams" have been "torn out and trucked away."

Perhaps no character represents West Virginians better than Ava, a woman who lives a hard life with a cruel husband. In the poem "May Apple." despite her "wilted celery looks," Ava "harvests may apples and bee balm/that she might boil a cloudy tea for his sore joints/his fireless blood." She hides peeled poplar branches beneath his pillow to cure him in his sleep. Readers assume "he" is her unloving husband who says in response to her plea for a child, "I'm not God." Yet Ava continues to try, "chooses/a pale whispery stuff to powder her forehead and cheeks,/a burnt red like the poppers she planted in a tire."

Historical references to West Virginia's role in the nation's history abound. "The Bird Collector," a prose poem about Alexander Wilson's 1810 trip to the Ohio River in search of birds, imagines the interaction between native people and the outsider Wilson. "In the Reformatory, Billie Holiday Refuses to Sing" depicts Holiday at the Federal Women's Reformatory at Alderson, West Virginia, where she served eight months in 1948.

Woolfitt also considers how locals reacted to poet Muriel Rukeyser's reporting on the Hawk's Nest Tunnel tragedy, in which nearly 2000 miners died from acute silicosis in the early 1930s while constructing the tunnel—an incident that many historians see as the worst industrial disaster in United States history. "Muriel scribbles diverted river, emptied bed,/ stagnant bed, the five mile section the townspeople call the dries." Yet, "The driller's wife believes, "paper deceives, she

Despite such humble circumstances, Woolfitt's characters still want beauty.

trusts word of mouth,/the Lord of hosts.../Scribble dry drill, dynamite." She mourns the tunnel's human ruin, her man said, "he had no choice," he coughs in the night and "bruises where she pressed him."

Walker Evans's photographs are the focus of "Interior Detail West Virginia Coal Miner's House," which details poverty and poor housing, but also the courage and hardiness of miners and their families. The description of the house suggests a miner's physical condition, where "walls hold up just barely/ hold up some of the panting."

Despite such humble circumstances, Woolfitt's characters still want beauty. One woman looks for a lost needle to complete a quilt pattern, as she struggles to "eke out a living here," patch the ceiling and make do with what she can, "her genius and industry patchworking the walls..."

Woolfitt's poetry relies on the senses, beauty juxtaposed with images of waste where, "The world is with me in cornea, cochlea, on tongues," "Like a defibrillated pacemaker, the risen dead" and declares, "My tongue has power enough to reform/or demolish; the earth is fruit for me when I take a bite." Indeed these poems are rich with the taste of earth as if in the language itself could restore the world.

In "Note to Slash Fires, to Draglines" the speaker's short sentences and clipped language acknowledge apathy. A realist, Woolfitt knows both the beauty and destruction in his native land, and like the speaker in "Home Remedies" who recounts a litany of home remedies interspersed with mourning a loved man at his wake, agrees that "he is not really here, " yet he "loves what's still here." ■

CONTRIBUTORS

Wiley Cash is the *New York Times* best-selling author of *A Land More Kind Than Home* and *This Dark Road to Mercy*. Cash teaches fiction at UNC-Chapel Hill and in the Low-Residency MFA Program in Fiction and Nonfiction Writing at Southern New Hampshire University. A native of North Carolina, he lives in Wilmington with his wife and their young daughter.

Amy Clark's writing has appeared or is forthcoming in the *New York Times,* NPR, *Still, Appalachian Heritage, Blue Ridge Country, Appalachian Journal,* and many other publications. Her co-edited book, *Talking Appalachian: Voices, Identity, and Community,* was used as a dialect resource for actors during the filming of *Big Stone Gap,* a movie adaptation of Adriana Trigiani's novel of the same title.

Laura Michele Diener moved to Huntington, West Virginia, seven years ago to teach history at Marshall University. She has discovered true love for her adopted home, although, like most loves, it is tinged with worry for the future. Her creative work has appeared in the *Catholic Worker, Lake Effect,* and *Cargo Lit.*

Renee Emerson is the author of *Keeping Me Still.* She earned her MFA in poetry from Boston University, where she was also awarded the 2009 Academy of American Poets Prize. She is also the author of three chapbooks of poetry: *Where Nothing Can Grow, The Whitest Sheets,* and *Something Like Flight.* Emerson teaches at Shorter University and lives in Northern Georgia with her husband and daughters.

D.A. Gray spends his time as a full-time graduate student at Texas A&M-Central Texas in the spring and fall, and as an MFA candidate at Sewanee School of Letters in the summer. He has published one book of poetry, *Overwatch,* and his work can also be found in *Grey Sparrow Journal, Bellow, Poetry Salzburg, The Good Men Project, O'Dark Thirty, 94 Creations,* and *Spark: A Creative Anthology.*

Dave Harrity's work has appeared in *Memorious, Revolver, Killing the Buddha, The Los Angeles Review, Confrontation, Softblow,* and elsewhere. His book of poems, *Our Father in the Year of the Wolf,* is forthcoming from WordFarm. Harrity teaches at Campbellsville University and lives in Louisville with his wife and family.

Holly Goddard Jones is the author of the novel *The Next Time You See Me* and the short story collection *Girl Trouble.* Her work has appeared in *The Best American Mystery Stories, New Stories from the South, Tin House,* and elsewhere. She teaches in the creative writing program at the University of North Carolina at Greensboro and lives with her husband, son, and two rowdy dogs.

Devin Kelly is an MFA student at Sarah Lawrence College where he serves as head nonfiction editor for *LUMINA Journal.* His poetry, fiction, and essays have appeared or are forthcoming in *Dunes Review, Catch & Release, Steel Toe Review, Cleaver Magazine,* and *Passages North.* He teaches creative writing and English classes to seventh graders and high schoolers in Queens, and teaches poetry workshops for the New York Public Library. He currently lives in Harlem.

Bill King is a 1990 graduate of the M.A. program in creative writing at the University of Georgia and teaches creative writing and literature at Davis & Elkins College in Elkins, West Virginia, where he directs the D&E Writers Series. His work has appeared or is forthcoming in A *Narrow Fellow: Journal of Poetry, Still, Wild Sweet Notes II: More Great Poetry from West Virginia, Nantahala, Flycatcher, The Southern Poetry Anthology (Georgia),* and other journals.

Courtney Mandryk holds an MFA in Poetry from the University of Michigan, where she received a Hopwood Award. Her work has appeared in journals such as *Adirondack Review, Michigan Quarterly Review,* and *Cream City Review.*

Sandra Marchetti is the author of *Confluence,* her debut full-length poetry collection. Eating Dog Press also published an illustrated edition of her essays and poetry, *A Detail in the Landscape,* and her first volume, *The Canopy,* won Midwest Writing Center's Mississippi Valley Chapbook Contest. Her work appears in *The Journal, Subtropics, Mid-American Review, Thrush Poetry Journal, South Dakota Review, Phoebe, Southwest Review,* and elsewhere.

Maren O. Mitchell's poems have appeared in *The South Carolina Review, Hotel Amerika, Southern Humanities Review, The Journal of Kentucky Studies, Appalachian Journal,* the anthologies *The Southern Poetry Anthology, V: Georgia, The Southern Poetry Anthology, VII: North Carolina,* and elsewhere. Her nonfiction book is *Beat Chronic Pain, An Insider's Guide* (Line of Sight Press, 2012). She lives with her husband in the Blue Ridge Mountains.

Christen Noel is a teacher and MFA candidate at Northern Michigan University where she's also an associate editor for *Passages North.* When she isn't writing, Noel can usually be found on the shores of Lake Superior with her dog, Dr. Watson. Her most recent work can be found in *Sugared Water, East Coast Literary Review,* and *The Rumpus.*

Heidi Siegrist lives and works as a freelance writer in Chicago, Illinois, where she stayed after graduating from the University of Chicago because she wasn't sure where else to go. She is also an MFA student at the University of the South in Sewanee, Tennessee, and is currently working on a collection of essays about our various human entanglements and how they're shaped by the places we can and can't return to.

Cheryl Smart is a second-year MFA candidate at the University of Memphis studying Creative Nonfiction. She is current Assistant Managing Editor and past Nonfiction Editor of the literary journal *The Pinch.* She has publications appearing or forthcoming in *The Little Patuxent Review, Cleaver Magazine, Word Riot, Apeiron Review,* and others. Smart is currently working on a collection of short stories and vignettes about her rural upbringing titled *Homespun.*

Natalie Sypolt lives and writes in West Virginia. She is an Assistant Professor at Pierpont Community and Technical College and also teaches community creative writing classes and workshops. Her work has appeared in *Glimmer Train, Switchback, r.kv.r.y., Ardor Literary Magazine, Superstition Review, Paste, Willow Springs Review,* and *The Kenyon Review Online.* Sypolt is the winner of the *Glimmer Train* New Writers Contest and the Betty Gabehart Prize.

Genevieve Thurtle lives in the San Francisco Bay Area with her husband and son. She received her MFA in Writing from Vermont

College of Fine Arts in July 2014. Her work has been published in *Crazyhorse* and *The Chariton Review*. She recently completed a short story collection entitled *Aphasia and Days*.

Meg Wilson is a photographer based in Paint Lick, Kentucky. She travels all over to make beautiful pictures of stories. Wilson credits her deep connection to her own family with her love of photographing other families, particularly on their wedding days. Her work has been featured in "Looking at Appalachia" and on her own website, www.blog.megwilsonphotography.com.

Sylvia Woods, a native of Clay County, Kentucky, lives in Oak Ridge, Tennessee, where she spent her youth teaching high school English. Her poetry has been published in journals and anthologies including *Appalachian Heritage, Now and Then, Motif, Southern Poetry Anthology III: Appalachia,* and *Southern Poetry Anthology VI: Tennessee.*